PASSOVER

JPS Popular Judaica Library
General Editor: Raphael Posner

PASSOVER

Edited by Mordell Klein

JEWISH PUBLICATION SOCIETY OF AMERICA
Philadelphia, Pa.

Copyright © Israel Program for Scientific Translations Ltd., 1973

First published in Israel by KETER BOOKS, an imprint of
ISRAEL PROGRAM FOR SCIENTIFIC TRANSLATIONS LTD.
P.O. Box 7145, Jerusalem

Published by
THE JEWISH PUBLICATION SOCIETY OF AMERICA
222 N. 15th St., Philadelphia, Pa. 19102

Library of Congress Catalogue Card 73 2880
ISBN 0 8276 0025 9

Printed in Israel

CONTENTS

INTRODUCTION

Special festive days add an element of excitement to life without which it would be monotonous. The Jewish calendar is well endowed with holydays — joyful and sad — which act as points of both expectation and departure throughout the annual cycle. The festivals are looked forward to with anticipation, and the experience they supply is savored after they have gone. In the rabbinic tradition, they are the generators from which man's spiritual batteries, his soul, should be recharged. Each festival tells its own story and carries a unique message which, according to the imagination of the celebrant, can be relevant to the situation in which he finds himself. The festivals are opportunities for us to elevate ourselves out of our humdrum existence by associating ourselves with an historic event and refining our sensitivities towards a higher and better life.

This is especially true for the festival of Passover which celebrates the most important and dramatic event in Jewish history, the Exodus from Egypt. This festival recalls the liberation of the Jewish people from slavery and points to an ultimate redemption for all mankind.

Passover is the most complicated of all the festivals. It requires a great deal of preparation and is absolutely distinctive in the way it is observed. The normal diet is completely changed and even different utensils are used. There is nothing even remotely resembling the *seder* night during the rest of the year. Notwithstanding the work involved in preparing for it, Passover is a very popular festival; it is observed, in some form or other, by more Jews than observe the other festivals. Everyone seems to find something in it.

In this book we have discussed, albeit very briefly, the historical setting of Passover, the manner in which it has been and is observed, and the promise it offers. We hope that the information and ideas in this book will help make the festival somewhat more meaningful for the reader; if it succeeds in that, even to a modest degree, it will have served its purpose.

עֲקֶרֶת הַבַּיִת אֵם הַבָּנִים
שְׂמֵחָה הַלְלוּיָהּ

מִצֵּאת

יִשְׂרָאֵל מִמִּצְרַיִם
בֵּית יַעֲקֹב מֵעַם לֹעֵז הָיְתָה
יְהוּדָה לְקָדְשׁוֹ יִשְׂרָאֵל

A medieval depiction of the Exodus scene. Moses is leading the Children of Israel out of the city gate. All participants are dressed in medieval costume. From the *Kaufmann Haggadah*, 14th Century, Spain.

1. WE WERE SLAVES TO PHARAOH IN EGYPT

Passover is the most ancient of all Jewish festivals. It is a national festival, an agricultural festival, and an extremely popular family festival that is celebrated every spring for a period of seven days (in Israel: eight in the Diaspora) on the anniversary of the Exodus from Egypt over three thousand years ago. The Exodus marks the birth of the Jewish nation, for the liberation from foreign domination and oppression was followed by national and religious independence.

Name
The name Passover (*Pesaḥ* in Hebrew) is connected with this event. The Bible records that a lamb had been ritually slaughtered by every Israelite household in Egypt and some of its blood smeared on their doorposts. At the sight of this blood, God "passed over (*pasaḥ* in Hebrew) the houses of the Children of Israel when He smote the Egyptians, and He delivered our houses. "The name *Pesaḥ* was subsequently given to the Paschal lamb that was to be sacrificed every year to commemorate that event and the festival was called *Ḥag ha-Pesaḥ*. In the Bible the festival also appears as *Ḥag ha-Maẓẓot* (The Feast of Unleavened Bread), since *maẓẓot* (unleavened bread) are eaten then. It is popularly known as *Ḥag he-Aviv,* since it is observed in the month of *Aviv* (spring) when the harvest is just beginning, and special ceremonies take place to mark this season.

History
The central activity of the Passover celebrations is the transmission of the story of the Exodus to future generations. Families congregate around a festive table on the first night of Passover, and in the course of a picturesque ceremony called the *seder,* parents perform the religious duty of telling their children the story of the national beginnings of their people.

1

The story of the Exodus is related not only as a record of historical facts, but also as an affirmation of belief in the future redemption and liberation of all Jews, regardless of their present situation. In fact, the story of how an oppressed people attained their freedom, and then of the yearning and striving to preserve and secure that state, and their constant affirmation of the right of men to be free, contains elements of universal relevance.

Dating the Exodus

The exact date of the Exodus is difficult to determine. The story, as told in the Bible, of a band of seventy Israelite shepherds who entered Egypt as Pharaoh's guests and who then remained to become slaves until their descendants were liberated by God through His prophet Moses, is not mentioned in other sources. Egyptian sources contain no direct references to these events which can hardly have passed unnoticed, though it was apparently the normal custom for the Egyptians to conceal their defeats.

According to Jewish tradition the Children of Israel left *Traditional* Egypt on Thursday the fifth of Nisan in the year 2248 *anno Dates mundi* (after the Creation), which corresponds to 1313 b.c.e. Other dates suggested in traditional sources are 1308, 1306, and 1280 b.c.e. Most archaeologists and historians however believe that the available evidence indicates one of the two following dates.

A passage in the First Book of Kings records: "And it came *1450-1430* to pass in the four hundred and eightieth year after the Children *b.c.e.* of Israel were come out of the land of Egypt, in the fourth year of Solomon's reign over Israel. . . . that he began to build the house of the Lord." Since Solomon reigned over Israel during the second half of the tenth century b.c.e., this would fix the Exodus between the years 1450 and 1430 b.c.e. Confirmation for this date appears to come in the Book of Judges which states that 300 years elapsed from the time of the Israelite entry into Canaan until the time that Jephthah was a judge in Israel, which was in the second half of the 12th century b.c.e. This early date

2

for the Exodus is also preferred by those scholars who are of the opinion that the *Habiru* mentioned in the Tell-el-Amarna letters, who penetrated Canaan and waged war against it, were in fact the Hebrews. The majority of scholars, however, reject this identification.

Most of the written or material evidence seems to point instead to the 13th century b.c.e. In the Book of Exodus we find: "And it came to pass at the end of four hundred and thirty years, even the selfsame day it came to pass, that all the hosts of the Lord went out from the land of Egypt." If we see the arrival of Jacob and his sons into Egypt as coinciding with that of the Hyksos whose capital Avaris or Zoan was built in about 1700 b.c.e., the date of the Exodus would be around 1270 b.c.e. This would make Ramses II the Pharoah of the enslavement, and he is known to have rebuilt the city of Per-Ramses in Wadi Tumeilat which may very well be the Ramses of "Pithom and Ramses" which, according to the Bible, the Israelites built. He was a well known builder, and he is known to have used foreign slaves some of whom are designated as *Apir,* a name rather like the word Hebrew. The Exodus could then have taken place during his reign, but definitely not later than the reign of his son Merneptah

The Merneptah Stele from Thebes (c.1230 b.c.e.) containing the only known use of the name "Israel" in ancient Egyptian writing. One passage reads: ". . . carried off is Ashkelon, seized upon is Gezer; Yanoam is made as that which does not exist; Israel is laid waste, his seed is not; Hurru is become a widow for Egypt! . . . . "

who was Pharaoh at the end of the 13th century b.c.e. The Merneptah stele, discovered in Thebes in 1896, contains the first direct Egyptian reference to the Israelites. "Israel is laid waste, his seed is not." In this boast of victory, which may in fact conceal defeat, the Egyptian determinative sign used is one for a people and not for a land, and so seems to indicate a nomadic people wandering about somewhere near Palestine.

Other factors also contribute to this later date being preferred. It appears that Transjordan was desolate between the 19th and 14th centuries. It was only at the beginning of the 13th century that the settlement of Ammonites, Moabites, and Edomites took place there, defended by a network of fortresses and strongholds. The Bible refers to these settlements.

Excavations at Hazor and Lachish also seem to indicate that their destruction took place at some time in the 13th century, which would then make the 13th century the date for Joshua's entry into the Promised Land.

Some scholars see a great similarity between the biblical story *The Hyksos* of the Israelites and what we know of the Hyksos.

The Hyksos were known to contemporary Egyptians as the *hekau khoswe*, "the rulers of foreign lands," they were a dynasty of Asiatics who infiltrated into the Nile Valley from Palestine over a period of several centuries. During the chaotic period which ended the Egyptian Middle Kindgom they managed to seize the kingship of Egypt, approximately between the years 1655 and 1580 b.c.e. They were initially expelled to Southern Palestine by Pharaoh Ahmes in 1580 b.c.e., and his successors later completed the expulsion. Josephus, the Jewish historian of the first century, quotes the Ptolemaic Egyptian writer Manetho who interpreted the name Hyksos to mean "king-shepherds" and also "captive shepherds." In his attempts to prove the antiquity of the Jews, Josephus goes on to connect the Hyksos with the Patriarchal Jews who were initially honored shepherds and later became captives, and he equates their appearance in Egypt with the Joseph story. He also equates the Exodus of the Israelites

4

with the subsequent expulsion of the Hyksos, partially following Manetho who was of the opinion that the expelled Hyksos together with a host of lepers were the founders of Jerusalem. Modern scholarship, however, sees absolutely no basis for this identification, although it is possible that the entry of the early Israelites into Egypt may have coincided with the period of Hyksos domination, and may have even been helped by it. Consequently their position in Egypt may have become greatly weakened by the departure of the Hyksos and as a result it was without much difficulty that the former honored guests were enslaved.

Abraham

The Bible thus remains the principal source for the story of the Exodus. Here the enslavement of the Israelites and their subsequent liberation is portrayed as the unfolding of a divine plan. The Book of Genesis records that after the patriarch Abraham had come to believe in the One God, he was designated as the founder of a nation who would hold similar beliefs, and who would be as numerous as the "stars of the heaven, and as the sand which is upon the sea-shore." However, before this would happen "thy seed shall be a stranger in a land that is not theirs, and shall serve them; and they shall afflict them four hundred years." Some commentators have expressed the opinion that this slavery in Egypt was a necessary factor in molding the Israelites together into becoming a free nation; shared suffering strengthens the bonds between people and unites their aspirations. They also view the humiliation and persecution that Jews have suffered throughout the ages as a prerequisite to their ultimate freedom.

Strangers in a Land not Theirs

The prediction made to Abraham that his seed would be strangers in a land that was not theirs began to be fulfilled when his grandson Jacob, who was also called Israel, took his whole clan

Episodes of the Joseph story from the *Golden Haggadah,* Barcelona, 1320.
Top right, Joseph's brothers kill a goat, stain Joseph's cloak with its blood,
and throw him into a pit. Top left, Joseph is sold to an Ishmaelite caravan
headed for Egypt. Bottom right, the stained cloak is shown to Jacob, who
tears his clothing in mourning. Bottom left, Potiphar's wife attempts to
seduce Joseph, and Joseph in jail with the King's chief butler and baker, in-
terpreting their dreams.

Detail from the *Golden Haggadah* showing the infant Moses being found in the river by Pharoah's daughter's handmaids.

of seventy persons down to Egypt to escape the famine in his native Canaan. They arrived in Egypt at the invitation of Jacob's son Joseph who was then the chief minister in charge of all food supplies in Egypt, the only country in the area where there was food.

The story of Joseph and his brothers is well known. They were jealous of him, and sold him as a slave to a caravan that was on its way to Egypt. There he served as a slave to an important family, and rose to a high position. The wife of his owner made amorous advances to him and, when these were rebuffed, she had him thrown in jail. Here he became known for his ability to interpret dreams and when nobody could interpret Pharoah's dream in which seven fat cows were eaten by seven lean ones, Joseph was called out of prison. He interpreted the dream as meaning that seven years of plenty were coming, to be followed by seven years of famine. Joseph was then entrusted with implementing the measures that he had suggested should be taken in preparation for this time. So when the entire area was stricken

Joseph

7

with famine there was food in Egypt, and Joseph was in charge of it.

The Book of Genesis relates in detail the story of Joseph's *Honored* reunion with his father and family in Egypt, and also of the *Guests* honor that was accorded to the family of the grand minister Joseph who had saved them all from starvation. They were invited to settle in the lush area of Goshen which is generally assumed to be located in Wadi Tumeilat which stretches from the eastern arm of the Nile to the Great Bitter Lake, and is known to be excellent pasture land. Jacob and his family of shepherds settled there. They prospered, and their numbers increased so much that "the land was filled with them."

Pharaoh saw the ever-increasing numbers of Israelites as con- *Enslavement* stituting a threat to Egypt. After Joseph died he made them slaves and mobilized them for his building programs. Yet the numbers of the Israelites continued to grow. In fact the Book of Exodus records that the slavery even spurred them on: "But the more they afflicted them, the more they spread abroad."

Pharaoh therefore introduced oppressive and then repressive *Oppression* measures. He commanded his people: "Every son that is born ye shall cast into the river;" the girls did not seem to present such a tangible threat. The rabbinic commentators also list a whole series of other harsh measures. The reaction of the enslaved Israelites was: "We cried to the Lord, the God of our fathers, and the Lord heard our voice."

Moses
Moses, an Israelite child, was saved from being drowned by being put into a basket and placed among the reeds of the Nile. He was found there by Pharaoh's daughter who took him from the water and brought him to the royal palace as her own son. It was this act, says the Bible, that gave Moses (*Moshe* in Hebrew) his name, for "it was from the water that I drew him out" (in Hebrew *meshitihu*). This derivation, however, relies more on assonance than etymology, and scholars see in the name Moses a parallel to

8

other Egyptian names such as Ptah-Mose (Ptah is born). They also see similarities in the story of Moses to the Egyptian myth which tells of the concealment by his mother of the infant-god, Horus, among the marsh-reeds to protect him from Seth. The story of an infant castaway who grows up to be a leader is a very popular legendary motif.

Despite his royal upbringing Moses could not evade the consequences of his identity, and he was drawn to bettering the lives of his less fortunate brothers. One day he could not restrain himself at the sight of an Israelite being harshly beaten by an Egyptian taskmaster, and he killed him. If discovered, his action would have serious consequences and, in fact, the Bible records that a fellow Israelite threatened to expose him. Moses fled into the desert. At the sight of a bush that was aflame but was not being consumed, he received a divine command to go back to Egypt to liberate the Israelites.

Moses was told by God to tell Pharaoh: "Let My people go!" However, Pharaoh was not to be impressed into losing his whole exploitable labor force so easily. On the contrary, he made the work harder, increased the quotas, and reduced the materials available to the people. As a consequence, Moses' own people, the people he was trying to liberate, turned on him and begged him to desist from his efforts; he was only making life more difficult for them.

Let My People Go

Moses standing before the burning bush, from a 13th cent. Spanish *Haggadah.* To the left is an angel.

9

Page from the 15th century *Joel ben Shimon Haggadah* with text of the Ten Plagues and miniature illustrations for each one which are to be read top to bottom (1st five) and right to left.

Moses, however, was carrying out a divine mission and when Pharaoh refused to release the Israelites, Egypt was stricken with plagues. The Bible gives us differing versions on the number and content of the plagues, but the version in the Psalms is usually attributed to poetic license.

Attempts have been made to interpret these plagues in terms of ancient Egyptian beliefs, as the humiliation of the gods of Egypt. *Hapi* the Nile-god, *Hekt* a frog-headed goddess, and *Re* the sun-god, all suffer at the hands of the God of Israel.

Others link these plagues to local or seasonal phenomena. The Nile may become reddened during its annual summer rise by organisms carried in it, and normally swarms of frogs and insects would follow this flooding; in fact insects were plentiful all year. Egyptian boils were proverbial, and hail, though uncommon, has been known to fall in January. Swarms of locusts may be blown across the country in winter or spring even nowadays. And the

A table of the Plagues of Egypt as they appear in biblical sources.

The Plagues

EXODUS	PSALM 78:44–51	PSALM 105:28–36
1. Blood Nile; all water; fish died	1. Blood Nile; liquids	1. Darkness
2. Frogs nuisance to men	2. Swarms[1] "consumed them"	2. Blood water; fish died
3. Lice nuisance to men and beats	Frogs "ruined them"	3. Frogs nuisance
4. Swarms[1] nuisance to men; ruined land	3. *Hasil*[2] ate produce	4. Swarms[1] } nuisance
5. Pestilence killed livestock	Locusts ate "toil"	Lice }
6. Boils pained men and beasts	4. Hail destroyed vines	5. Hail } destroyed vines, figs, trees
7. Hail and fire destroyed plants, men and beasts	*Hanamel*[3] destroyed sycamores	Fire }
8. Locusts destroyed plants	5. Hail[4] destroyed beasts	6. Locusts } destroyed all vegetation
9. Darkness immobilized men	*Reshafim*[5] destroyed livestock	*Yeleq*[2] }
10. Firstborn death	6. Death } killed men[6] Pestilence }	7. Firstborn death
	7.[7] Firstborn death	

[1] Heb. '*arov*; LXX: "dogflies"; R. Nehemiah (Ex. R.) "gnats and mosquitoes"; NJPS "swarms of insects." But Josephus (Ant. 2: 303), R. Judah (Ex. R.), and Targ. "mixture of birds and beasts."
[2] A kind (or stage of development) of locusts.
[3] Meaning obscure; LXX: "frost"; medieval conjectures: "locust," "stones".
[4] Symmachus: "pestilence" (*dever* for MT *barad*).
[5] Traditionally "fiery bolts", but *Reshef* is a Canaanite plague-god, and *reshef* in Deuteronomy 32:24 (|| *qetev*) and Habakkuk 3:5 (|| *dever*) means "pestilence" (cf. note 4)
[6] *Hayyatam* = *nafsham*, "their life" (Ibn Ezra; cf. Rashi). LXX, Targ. misconstrue as "their beasts".
[7] Ibn Ezra joins to the preceding.

darkness that is mentioned as **being so thick** that it could **be felt,** seems to be very much like the heavy sandstorms that are raised by the *ḥamsin* winds that blow in the early spring. In this view, the miracle of these plagues was that these phenomena appeared more intensified and concentrated, and at a very opportune time.

Yet despite the plagues, Pharaoh remained adamant in his refusal to release the Israelites; God had "hardened his heart." The Book of Exodus gives us here a very clear picture of the two-level biblical view of history. Human events are shaped by the will of God, yet they unfold in accordance with the motives of the actors who do God's will, thinking it their own. However, the tenth plague in which all the Egyptian firstborn were to die, threatened Pharaoh's own family and even his life. At this, he capitulated. In the middle of the night he ordered the Israelites out of Egypt, whether they desired their freedom or not. *A Hardened Heart*

In Haste from Egypt
Every Israelite household had slaughtered a lamb as they had been commanded. According to commentators, this was an act of faith because the lamb was a holy animal for the Egyptians who could be expected to be provoked in rather the same way that Hindus in India are when Muslims there slaughter cows. They had sprinkled some of the lamb's blood on their door-posts, and were eating the lambs with their families, with their "loins girded" ready to depart. Thus as soon as they heard Pharaoh's command, they hastened out of Egypt. There was not even time for the dough to rise and as a result they ate *mazzah.*

The Book of Exodus relates that about 600,000 men, besides women and children, left Egypt. Some rabbinic commentators believe that this is a rather conservative number, whereas critical scholars are inclined to see it as an exaggeration, claiming that it is hardly likely that an exodus of such a large number of people should have gone unmentioned in Egyptian records. David Ben-Gurion, the first prime minister of the modern State of Israel and a keen Bible student, nearly provoked a cabinet crisis with his *600,000*

A double page from the *Second Nuremberg Haggadah,* with marginal illustrations of the Exodus. The Israelites are depicted as armed soldiers, on horseback and on foot. Germany, 15th cent.

religious coalition-partners when he claimed that the number of people leaving Egypt at the time of the Exodus was probably not more than 600 families.

As many as they were, the Children of Israel set off for the Promised Land. The shortest route would have been through Sila which is near Qantarah, then on to El-Arish, Rafiah and Gaza. But "God did not lead them by way of the land of the Philistines, although that was near; for God said, 'Lest the people repent when they see war, and return to Egypt.'" The people had been slaves for so long they were not psychologically prepared for war. The Martinique psychologist Franz Fanon, who practised in Algeria during their War of Independence, and who

Without Violence

13

studied the psychology of colonized peoples, would have appreciated this reasoning. However, he would have insisted that it is only through violence that those who have been suppressed by force can overcome their sense of inferiority. Ibn Ezra, the renowned Bible commentator of the 12th century, remarked that for this reason the former slaves had to die in the wilderness; only the new generation could fight for the Promised Land.

Consequently a circuitous route was taken. The names of the places on the route are noted in the Bible, but they are not easily identifiable. There are four main theories for the route from Egypt to Kadesh Barnea, and there are two main theories for the route of their journey from Kadesh Barnea to the Moabite plateau. Two reconstructed maps are shown. *The Route*

After leaving Egypt the Israelites marched forward to freedom. However, by morning Pharaoh had regretted his hasty decision. He set out with his well-equipped army to bring them back. He was sighted by them at the Sea of Reeds. Since the time of the translation of the Bible into Greek in the third century b.c.e. it was generally accepted that the sea referred to here was the Red Sea, and that the crossing took place in the vicinity of Suez. However, the majority of scholars nowadays identify this sea with one of the lagoons on the shores of the Mediterranean. Be that as it may, there was a sea in front of the Children of Israel and behind them was Pharaoh. Moses raised his staff and the waters parted. The Israelites passed through safely; "the waters were a wall to them on their right hand and on their left." But as the Egyptians followed them through, "the waters returned and covered the chariots and the horsemen and all the host." *The Sea of Reeds*

The Midrash permits us to eavesdrop on a conversation between God and the angels who wished to sing a song of praise to Him for having performed such a miracle to save His people. God refused: "The work of My hands is drowning in the sea, and you want to chant a victory song before Me!" How can one be fully happy when others are suffering, even deservedly? The Children *The Song of the Sea*

14

Map showing two theories as to
the route by the tribes from Kadesh
Barnea to the Plains of Moab (left).

Map showing some of the theories
on the route of the Exodus from
Egypt to Kadesh-Barnea, one of the
major stopping points on the route
to Canaan. In addition, some of the
important sites are given, also according to various theories. Note the
nine suggested locations for Mount
Sinai.

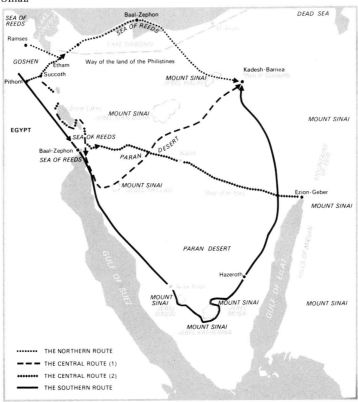

of Israel, however, had just been saved, and they could not restrain themselves:

> "I will sing to the Lord, for He is highly exalted;
> the horse and his rider hath He thrown into the sea.
> The Lord is my strength and song,
> and He is become my salvation."

The "Song of the Sea," as this paean of praise is known, has become a part of the daily liturgy, and the Sabbath on which that portion of the Pentateuch is publicly read in the synagogue is considered a special festive Sabbath. The song is also read from the Torah on the seventh day of Passover, the anniversary of the event.

After the Egyptians had drowned, there was no possibility that the Israelites would lose their newly-won independence; they had now attained physical freedom, the time had come for spiritual liberation. They journeyed to Mount Sinai and encamped there.

In the accompanying maps one can see at least nine places *Mount Sinai* that have been identified as Mt. Sinai, and there are many more which are not shown. There is no Jewish tradition of the actual geographical location of Mt. Sinai; rabbinic literature was always more concerned with the content and ideas of the Torah than with the question of where it was given. For it was at Mount Sinai that the Children of Israel were to receive the Torah which was to provide the legal and spiritual framework for all future generations of Jews.

"I am the Lord thy God who brought thee out of the land of Egypt, out of the house of slaves;" liberation by God required belief in Him, and that belief was to be manifested in obedience to the divine will. It is psychologically true that in personal relationships, doing things for the beloved enriches one's love. Aware of this, Jews have constantly stressed the need for the observance of ritual.

16

The generation that received the Torah perished in the wilderness, but their children did enter the Promised Land. They would never forget that the Exodus from Egypt, was the central event of their national history, and they have commemorated this event by observing the festival of Passover.

2. IN ORDER THAT YOU SHOULD REMEMBER

Celebrations were held in Egypt even before the Exodus had taken place; in fact these were to be the model for future Passovers. The sacrifice of the Paschal lamb was the central part of these celebrations. The Bible records how Moses transmitted God's injunctions to the Children of Israel: "Draw out, and take you lambs according to your families, and kill the Passover lamb." The lamb was slaughtered at dusk on the night of the fourteenth of the month of Nisan, and some of its blood was to be smeared on the doorposts of the Israelite houses so that God should pass over them when He smote the firstborn of Egypt. Instructions were also given as to how the lamb was to be eaten: "They shall eat the flesh in that night, roast with fire and unleavened bread; with bitter herbs shall they eat it. . . . . And thus shall ye eat it; with your loins girded, your shoes on your feet and your staff in your hand; and ye shall eat it in haste — it is the Lord's Passover."

These rites were also to be observed by future generations as a reminder of this occasion: "And it shall come to pass, when ye be come to the land which the Lord will give you, according as He hath promised, that ye shall keep this service. And it shall come to pass when your children shall say unto you, 'What mean ye by this service? ' that ye shall say, 'It is the sacrifice of the Lord's Passover, for that He passed over the houses of the children of Israel in Egypt when He smote the Egyptians and delivered our houses.' "

Passover Before the Exodus

However, some critical scholars claim that these rites pre-date the Exodus, and that the festival of Passover is in effect a combina- tion of two distinct festivals that were observed long before the Israelites became enslaved in Egypt, and that it was only con- nected to this historical event much later. They isolate the fes- tival of the sacrificial lamb, with its accompanying rituals such as smearing the blood on the door-post, as a festival that was ob- served by transient breeders to secure protection for their flocks before leaving their winter quarters at the arrival of spring. The feast of unleavened bread is seen as a pastoral festival which involved the first fruits of the land and which can be traced to the Canaanites; this was also observed by the patriarchs who were only semi-nomadic.

The Midrash tells us that the patriarch Abraham observed all the commandments, including Passover. In fact it was on Pass- over that the three angels came to visit him to bring him the news that despite the fact that he was a hundred years old and Sarah his wife was over ninety, they would soon have a child, Isaac. Abraham hurriedly prepared for them a meal of freshly slaugh- tered meat, and *mazzah* (unleavened bread) that Sarah had baked. According to the Midrash, Abraham's nephew Lot was also eating *mazzah* when the angels came to warn him to evacuate the area because of the impending destruction of Sodom and Gomorrah. A song in the *Haggadah* alludes to these incidents.

In the Wilderness

However, it was on the first anniversary of the Exodus from Egypt, when the Israelites were in the wilderness, that Passover, as an historical festival, was celebrated for the first time, in order "that thou mayest remember the day when thou camest forth from the land of Egypt all the days of thy life." The Book of Numbers relates: "they kept the Passover in the first month, on the fourteenth day of the month, at dusk, in the wilderness of

Sinai." There is no reference here to their having eaten the Paschal sacrifice or even unleavened bread or bitter herbs, but rabbinic commentators assume that they must have.

There is every reason to believe that Passover was not celebrated again after this until the Israelites arrived at their destination, Canaan. Uncircumcised males were not permitted to partake of the Paschal sacrifice, and "in the same way that a man's being uncircumcised prevents him from offering the Paschal sacrifice or eating from it, so the fact that his sons and his male servants are uncircumcised prevents him," for it was to be eaten in family groups. Tradition relates that whilst Pharaoh's suppressive measures of killing all newly-born boys were in force, the Jews refrained from having children. As regards the boys born after the liberation, travel in the wilderness and its accompanying hazards prevented them from being circumcised.

In the Promised Land

Shortly after the Israelites crossed the river Jordan, Joshua had all the men circumcised at Gilgal, a place whose name literally means "roll": for "this day have I rolled away the reproach of Egypt from off you." The "reproach of Egypt" probably refers to the inability of the Israelites to observe the Passover, and thus to their disregard of their freedom festival. After they were circumcised, "they kept the Passover on the fourteenth day of the month at evening in the plains of Jericho."

Detail from the *Golden Haggadah* showing the slaughter and preparation of the Paschal sacrifice.

19

In the First Temple

The Israelites entered the Promised Land, conquered it by stages and settled in it. Eventually King David captured Jerusalem and his son Solomon in c. 1000 b.c.e. built a Temple for the glory of God. According to the Book of Chronicles which was written much later, the appropriate sacrifices were offered up on all the required days, and also "on the appointed seasons, three times in the year, even in the Feast of Unleavened Bread. . . ." After Solomon's death the kingdom divided into two, the North and the South. Jerusalem and the Temple were in the Southern kingdom of Judah.

There are no further references to Passover in the Bible until the time of Hezekiah who ascended the throne of Judah in 726 b.c.e. The silence of the Bible does not necessarily mean that the festival was not observed, for the Bible records only historical events relevant to its purpose; yet we do know that there was much idolatry in those times. In fact, Hezekiah found it necessary to have the Temple rededicated after the paganism of the reigns of his predecessors. Afterwards "he sent to all Israel and Judah, and wrote letters also to Ephraim and Manasseh, that they should come to the house of the Lord at Jerusalem, to keep the Passover unto the Lord, the God of Israel." Despite the fact that the northern tribes of Israel constituted a separate kingdom and were at that time hard pressed by the Assyrians, who later conquered them and put an end to the Northern kingdom in 721 b.c.e., Hezekiah tried to use the Passover celebrations at Jerusalem as a means of uniting all the Jewish people. In much the same way there are Muslims nowadays, especially Arab Muslims, who would like to see the annual pilgrimage to Mecca become no longer just "a passport to heaven after a long life" but "a great political power." Hezekiah's ambition, though more limited, was similar. When the celebrations were held "there assembled at Jerusalem much people to keep the feast of unleavened bread in the second month, a very great congregation." However, the king was only partially successful; very few came from the North.

Hezekiah

20

These celebrations had been postponed to the second month, because the number of priests who were ritually clean at the proper date had not been adequate. However, when it was celebrated, it was "with great gladness; and the Levites and the priests praised the Lord day by day, singing with loud instruments unto the Lord."

Hezekiah's political motive for the celebration has caused some scholars to question the authenticity of this story. There is no mention in the Book of Kings of this Passover being celebrated; and the Book of Chronicles where this story appears was written at some time between 400 and 250 b.c.e., and may well have been trying to prove that the central shrine of Jerusalem was revered in earlier times by the Northern as well as the Southern Kingdom.

The celebration that took place in the time of Hezekiah's *Josiah* great-grandson, Josiah, king of Judah from 631-601 b.c.e., which is recorded in the Book of Kings, is accepted by all as having taken place. In the 18th year of his reign a copy of the Book of the Law was discovered, which some believe was the Book of Deuteronomy, and he read it to the assembled people. They immediately repented from their idol-worshipping and, after he had all the idolatry removed and the Temple purified, he commanded all the people: "Keep the Passover unto the Lord your God as it is written in this book of the covenant." With the festive crowds estimated at a minimum of 300,000 people — Josiah himself provided 30,000 lambs and kids for the Passover sacrifices and we reckon at least 10 persons to a lamb — an incomparable Passover was observed in 621 b.c.e.: "For there was not kept such a Passover from the days of the judges that judged Israel, nor in all the days of the kings of Israel, nor of the kings of Judah."

The Returning Exiles
Jerusalem was invaded and the Temple destroyed in 586 b.c.e. by the Babylonians. The population was exiled to Babylon, by

whose rivers they were to sit and weep as they remembered Zion. After an exile of seventy years they were allowed to return by decree of Cyrus the Persian who had conquered the Babylonians. So in 515 b.c.e. "the Children of Israel that were come back out of the captivity, and all such as had separated themselves unto them from the filthiness of the nations of the land to seek the Lord, the God of Israel, did eat, and kept the feast of unleavened bread seven days with joy."

The Second Temple was built and the process of centralizing the cult which had been encouraged by Hezekiah and Josiah made Jerusalem the focus of the Passover celebrations.

In Elephantine
Jerusalem was not, however, the only place in which Passover was celebrated. The first non-biblical sources that refer to the observance of Passover are the Elephantine papyri that were discovered at the beginning of this century. Elephantine is situated at the southern end of a small island in the Nile, and from at least the 5th century b.c.e. it was the site of a large camp of mercenaries which included companies of Jewish soldiers. These Jewish mercenaries had their own temple in which they worshipped the God of Israel, as well as other gods. Two ostraca and one papyrus have been found containing injunctions concerning Passover. In the rather imperfect text of the papyrus, which is a letter to the community, there is an instruction that "from the 15th day to the 21st day....be ye clean and take heed. Work not...you shall not drink, and anything at all leaven do not...." This letter is dated in the fifth year of Darius II, which was 419 b.c.e.

The Haggadah Censored
Parts of the *Haggadah* are very ancient, and as such may be used as an historical source, since the text bears the imprint of the changing political scene during the time of the Second Temple. The recounting of the story of the oppression and slavery in

Egypt and the subsequent victorious liberation could prove very embarrassing if Jews were again ruled by Egypt. During the years 301-198 b.c.e., Erez Israel was, in fact, under the domination of the Ptolemids of Egypt, who entrusted the rule to the family of the High Priest. At Passover, the Jews would diplomatically modify the passages which referred to Israel's liberation from Egyptian domination. Thus we find that in the passage quoted from Deuteronomy — "We were slaves to Pharaoh in Egypt" — the *Haggadah* continues, "And the Lord brought us forth from there. . . . " instead of "from Egypt. . . ", in case one should understand the verse as meaning from Egyptian domination wherever it may be. This verse has also been amputated, since it refers, in the source, to the severity of the Egyptians' defeat, and all references to Egyptian humiliation were avoided.

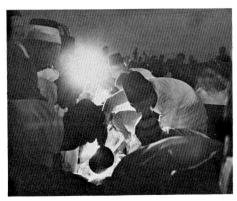

The Samaritan sacrifice of the Paschal lamb on Mt.Gerizim, 1968. The sheep is being plucked with the aid of boiling water.

An attempt was also made to underplay Jewish connections with Syria, Egypt's rivals for power in the area. The phrase "A wandering Aramean (Syrian) was my father," which refers to Jacob, was interpreted to mean "An Aramean tried to kill my father," so he went down to Egypt to seek protection from those Syrian killers. However, the reverse process was necessary when the Seleucids of Syria gained control over Erez Israel in the years 198-167 b.c.e. Emphasis was then laid on the passage, "Your fathers dwelt of old time beyond the River, even Terah, the father of Abraham. . . . " They were thus able to show the Syrians that they had affinities with them, and should be treated accordingly.

The Crucifixion of Jesus

The Syrians were driven out from Jerusalem by the Maccabees in 165 b.c.e., and an independent Jewish commonwealth was again set up under the Hasmoneans. However, only a hundred years later Jerusalem was again entered by foreign armies. In 63 b.c.e. the Roman general Pompey entered Jerusalem with his army to support one of the quarreling successors to the Hasmonean throne. Despite the Roman occupation, the Passover celebrations still continued. The New Testament records that in Jesus' youth "it was the practice of his parents to go to Jerusalem every year for the Passover festival; and when he was twelve, they made the pilgrimage as usual." It was also to a Roman-occupied Jerusalem that Jesus came to celebrate what was to be his last Passover. In fact, according to the Synoptic gospels, the Last Supper, during which the salvational significance of Jesus' death became clear and which was interrupted by Roman soldiers coming to take him away, was the Paschal meal. Jesus was thus crucified on the 15th of Nisan, the first day of Passover, in a Jerusalem crowded with people celebrating the festival. However, the Gospel of John moves the crucifixion forward to the 14th of Nisan, the eve of Passover, and thereby equates the death of Jesus with the slaughter of the sacrificial Paschal lamb.

Detail of the sculptured frieze from the left-hand entrance to the Church of the Holy Sepulchre in Jerusalem showing the Last Supper. The frieze dates from the Crusader period.

24

Passover of Dense Throngs

Jerusalem was usually crowded during Passover for two principal reasons. Firstly, after the Temple was built the Paschal sacrifices were not to be brought elsewhere. Secondly, there was the duty of pilgrimage: "Three times in the year all thy males shall appear before the Lord God," Passover was one of these times. Concerning this biblical commandment, the rabbis taught: "Whoever performs the duty of the pilgrimage is to be considered as if he had received the *Shekhinah*, the Divine Presence." As mentioned above, at least 300,000 people participated in the Passover ceremony during the reign of Josiah in 621 b.c.e. The Talmud relates that Agrippa I, who was king of Judea from 41-44 c.e., once took a census of the people by having the kidneys removed from the Paschal sacrifices. Over 600,000 pairs of kidneys were counted, and this became known as the "Passover of dense throngs." Josephus estimated that the number of Jews gathered in Jerusalem for the last Passover before the war in 70 c.e. was 3,000,000.

Pilgrimage to Jerusalem

Jews came from far and wide, from all over Erez Israel and even from the Diaspora, to be in Jerusalem during these festivals. Even nowadays Passover is a very popular season with tourists. However, in those days the visitors did not need the many hotels that are now mushrooming in Jerusalem; the Jerusalemites accommodated many of the visitors, not even taking rent from them, because this city was considered to be the common possession of the entire Jewish people. It was however the custom for the pilgrims to leave their hosts the hides of the sacrificial animals in gratitude.

Those who did not find accommodation in the city stayed in adjoining villages, or encamped in tents in the surrounding fields. Although Jerusalem was very crowded, "nobody ever said in Jerusalem: 'This place is too cramped for me.'" Some rabbis point out that they did not say this, even though they may very well have felt it — but there was a convivial atmosphere. Likewise, "nobody ever had occasion to say to his neighbor, 'I have been unable to find a stove for cooking the Paschal meal in Jerusalem.' "

Even after the Paschal meal had been completed, the pilgrims would linger on, utilizing the opportunity for *Torah* study, whilst they were in the central city. They would of course temper this with elaborate festive meals and celebrations.

The Paschal Sacrifice
The central event of the Passover celebrations in Temple times was the Paschal sacrifice. To commemorate the lamb consumed at the first Passover meal in Egypt, a Paschal sacrifice consisting of a lamb or kid-goat was to be slaughtered and eaten festively on that night every year by every Jewish household. On the eve of Passover the lambs or kid-goats were brought to the Temple, and slaughtered in the forecourt. Whereas other sacrifices were brought by individuals, this sacrifice was unique in that it was brought by groups and was to be eaten in its entirety before dawn by the group that brought it. The group usually consisted of all the members of a household, but "if the household be too little for a lamb, then shall he and his neighbor next unto his house take one according to the number of souls." Aliens and the uncircumcised could not be included in these groups. Because of the number of Paschal sacrifices that were brought, the Temple service was re-arranged to accommodate them, and the times of other offerings were brought forward. The proceedings would start at midday on the fourteenth of Nisan. First of all, the people were divided into three groups. When the first group had filled the Temple court, its gates were closed and the *shofar* was sounded. The Israelites would then slaughter their lambs, and the priests who were standing in rows in front of them would catch the sacrificial blood in the gold or silver bowls that they were holding. They would then pass these bowls on to the other

priests behind them, and the priest nearest the altar would sprinkle the blood in one motion against the base of the altar.

During the ceremony, the Levites chanted *Hallel* (Psalms 113-118). When this ceremony was over, the entire process was repeated for the second and third groups. The animals were then roasted whole, and care was taken to ensure that no bone was broken. After nightfall, every animal was eaten by the company which had brought it. The celebrants tried to ensure that none of it remained till the morning; whatever did remain, was burnt.

At the festive Passover meal during which the story of the Exodus was narrated and discussed, the Paschal sacrifice was eaten together with *mazzot* and bitter herbs. Nothing at all was to be eaten after it. The Mishnah enjoins: "After the Passover meal no *afikoman* is to be added;" the word *afikoman* here probably means dessert. The Passover meal was not to be eaten merely to satisfy hunger, but was to be savored so that the taste would linger. Nowadays a piece of *mazzah* known as the *afikoman* is eaten at the *seder* as a symbolic reminder of the Paschal meal, and it is the last food eaten that night. Sephardi celebrants still say: "In memory of the Paschal meal that was eaten when satiated."

The offering of the Paschal sacrifice required that a person be *Second* ritually pure. If he was impure during the time that the sacrifice *Passover* was to be brought, or he was in the middle of a long journey, he had another opportunity to fulfill this obligation a month later on the 14th of Iyyar, known as the Second or Minor Passover. That day is still known by the name of Second Passover, and is considered a minor festival; some people make a point of eating *mazzah* on it. Interestingly, if the whole populace was found to be ritually unclean, that uncleanness did not delay the sacrifice, and they would offer up their Paschal offerings in Jerusalem on the first Passover.

After The Destruction
After the Second Temple was destroyed by the Romans in 70

27

Pilgrims to Jerusalem carrying the Torah (under the canopy) to the Western
Wall on one of the intermediate days of Passover.

c.e., the Passover sacrifice could no longer be brought. There
were some, however, who argued that the Paschal sacrifice should
still be offered in Jerusalem even without the Temple. This controversy has been revived in modern times.

Although the Temple, the focal point of Jewish worship, was
destroyed, the rabbis ensured that Jewish religious practice
would continue. They stressed the idea that every man was to
turn himself into a temple; prayers were to be offered up instead
of sacrifices. Passover continued to be observed as the Feast of
Unleavened Bread during which *mazzah* was the only bread
which was permitted, and all *hamez* (leaven) was to be removed.
The Exodus from Egypt was remembered at the *seder* ceremony

28

Ram's horn blown on Mt. Zion, Passover, 1958, accompanying the pilgrims' ascent to the holiest site accessible for Jews before the liberation of the Temple Mount in the Six Day War, 1967.

on the first night, at which unleavened bread and bitter herbs were eaten, and the story of the Exodus was narrated. As the *seder* ceremony became crystallized a text was compiled to be read at it — the *Haggadah*.

Thus Jews continued to observe Passover throughout the ages. Wherever they were, and in whatever situation they found themselves, Jews remembered that their ancestors had been slaves in Egypt. For the 1900 years that they were without a homeland of their own, Jews were persecuted and Passover, especially in Christian countries, was a particularly difficult time since it always occurred near Easter, and also because of the blood-libel allegations which were quite a frequent occurrence from the 12th century. Yet many accounts testify that Jews did not cease observing Passover, even at the risk of their lives.

The complex of deliberate lies, trumped-up accusations and popular beliefs about the blood lust of the Jews, based on the concept that Jews hate Christianity and mankind in general, has a long history. The early Christians themselves suffered such accusations because of the holy bread of communion, about which it was believed that the divine child was in the bread that was being eaten. But it was Christians who were to prove to be the greatest of the persecutors of the Jews in this matter. They claimed that Jews seized and tortured innocent Christian children so as to repeat the passion and crucifixion of Jesus. This explains why so many of these accusations were made at Easter. They also claimed that Jews were not human and so needed special remedies such as human blood to appear like other men. Passover 1144 was apparently the date of the first ritual-murder accusations made in Norwich, England. From then on the libel appeared in all parts of Europe, leading to cruel massacres of Jews. The delusion that Christian blood was needed for the baking of the *mazzot* for Passover, was a motif that came increasingly to the fore in the 14th century. Russia was the scene of many such accusations in the 19th century; the book and then the film "The Fixer" were based on the actual case of a Jew, Jacob Beilis, who in 1911 was falsely accused of murdering a Christian child to use the blood for *mazzah*. The blood-libel was even imported into the Muslim-Arab East in the 19th century by zealous Christians. The Nazis were also to play on this theme. Himmler sent agents throughout Europe to collect so-called evidence, filling whole archives with reports on alleged ritual murder by Jews.

It is not surprising, therefore, that when the doors were opened at the *seder*, Jews should say with feeling: "Pour out Thy wrath upon the nations who knew Thee not. . . Pursue them with Wrath and destroy them from under the heavens of the Lord."

Despite the danger, however, the *seder* was not discontinued, nor even suspended; the story had to be told.

The scale of the persecutions which the Jews suffered in the 20th century was unprecedented. Yet even in the death camps of the Nazis the *seder* was still performed, even if only a small crust of bread was available; while themselves enslaved, Jews remembered how their ancestors had been liberated.

There were some whom Passover inspired to free themselves from such subjection. Passover 1943 was celebrated in the Warsaw Ghetto with a defiant yet hopeless revolt against the Nazis.

"Pesaḥ has come to the Ghetto again.
The lore-laden words of the Seder are said,
And the Cup of the Prophet Elijah awaits.
But the Angel of Death has intruded, instead.
As always — the German snarls his commands.
As always — the words sharpened up and precise.
As always — the fate of more Jews in his hands:
Who shall live, who shall die, this Passover night.
But no more will Jews to the slaughter be led.
The truculent jibes of the Nazis are past.
And the lintels and doorposts tonight will be red
With the blood of free Jews who will fight to the last."

3. THIS NIGHT ONLY MAẒẒAH

Passover is a festival which abounds in ritual. Much of this ritual is mentioned in the Torah, was amplified later by the rabbis, and then expanded by local custom. Some of these practices revolve specifically around the *seder* ceremony, while others apply for the whole duration of the festival; some of them also require advance preparation.

Duration
Passover commences on the 15th of Nisan and lasts for seven days; in the Diaspora eight days are observed. This additional day

was added before the calendar was fixed by advance calculation. The Jewish calendar is a lunar one, and in ancient times the position of the moon needed to be observed in order to determine when the new month would start. The position of the moon in Erez Israel each month then determined whether the 30th or the 31st day of the month would be the first day of the new month. The court in Jerusalem would hear the evidence of those who had seen the new moon, and their decision would then be broadcast to other places by an elaborate system of bonfires and messengers. There were often delays in this news arriving to distant places, and so there were often doubts as to whether the 30th or the 31st day of the old month had been declared as the first day of the new month. An extra day was therefore added to the three pilgrim festivals out of doubt, and this was preserved even after the calendar was fixed. In a lunar year there are only 354 days as compared to 365¼ in a solar year. The two years are synchronized by the addition of a month in each of the seven leap years that occur in every nineteen-year cycle. Thus Passover always occurs in spring in Israel and the northern hemisphere. The fixed calendar also ensures that the first day of Passover occurs only on certain days of the week.

In Israel the first and last days of Passover are "holy days" on which all work is prohibited, and the five intermediate days are "semi-holy" days on which necessary work is permitted. In the Diaspora the first two and last two days are "holy days," and the remaining four intermediate days are "semi-holy."

The Feast of Unleavened Bread

Passover is also referred to in the Bible as *Hag ha-Mazzot* — The Feast of Unleavened Bread. On the first night of the festival one is obliged to eat *mazzah* (unleavened bread), and in fact throughout Passover *mazzah* is the only type of bread which may be eaten. For the entire duration of the festival no *hamez* at all may be eaten, nor may there be even the most minute particle of *hamez* in any Jew's possession throughout the festival. The source for these injunctions is in the Book of Exodus: "Seven days shall ye eat unleavened bread; howbeit the first day ye shall put away leaven out of your houses; for whosoever eateth leavened bread (Hebrew, *ḥameẓ*) from the first day until the seventh day, that soul shall be cut off from Israel."

Ḥameẓ

Only that which actually ferments on decomposition is regarded as *ḥameẓ* (leaven). This law applies to five species of grain: wheat, barley, spelt, rye and oats. Any other fermentation is permitted. Grains which rot but do not ferment such as rice and millet are not in this category, and are therefore permitted on Passover. However, in practice, the only flour used by Ashkenazi communities is *mazzah* meal (ground *mazzah*) and potato flour. The Ashkenazi halakhic authorities felt that the use of rice and its flour in ways that in themselves were permitted on Passover, would confuse people who might use the same methods for grains which could become leaven. They therefore forbade the use of all *kitniyot* (pulse), a term which includes rice and millet; they even extended this prohibition to include "doubtful *kitniyot*" such as beans, peas, maize and peanuts. Our first record of this prohibition is from a 13th-century work which states that it was already widespread in those days. However the Sephardi communities never accepted this "fence around the law," and they do eat rice and beans on Passover.

Ḥameẓ which is prohibited on Passover is classified into three categories of descending stringency. *Three Categories*

Ḥameẓ Gamur is that which is completely *ḥameẓ*, and includes the fermented doughs of the five types of grain mentioned above, and also their derivatives, such as whiskey, that have fermented. It is reckoned that under normal conditions it takes about 18 minutes for flour mixed with water to begin fermenting.

Ta'arovet Ḥameẓ is something with even the slightest amount of *ḥameẓ* mixed in it.

Ḥamez Nuksheh is *ḥamez* that is hard and unfit for consumption; writer's paste is an example. This type of *ḥamez*, unlike the former two, may be kept on Passover but, of course, not eaten.

Minute Amounts

Many foods are forbidden to Jews by the *halakhah* all year round, and if a piece of one of them should fall into some other permitted food, the whole mixture would be forbidden. However, if such a mixture has come about accidentally, and the volume of the permitted food in the mixture is at least 60 times that of the forbidden food, the latter becomes nullified and the mixture is permitted; the taste of the forbidden food is said to have disappeared in the greater volume. There are several important qualifications to the law of nullification, but in general it is as stated. This law also applies to *ḥamez* that falls into food before Passover; on Passover itself no amount of *ḥamez* at all can be nullified in this way. Consequently even the minutest amount of *ḥamez* will render a mixture forbidden.

"Under Supervision"

As a result of this, practically every food product which has not been specially prepared so as to ensure that it does not contain the minutest amount of *ḥamez,* is forbidden on Passover. Traditional Jews are careful to use only food which has been prepared "under supervision" and pronounced "Kosher for Passover" by a recognized authority.

Preparation of utensils (*kashering*) for Passover by immersion in boiling water. Illustration from a 14th cent. *Haggadah* from Spain.

34

Kashering utensils in the Mea Shearim quarter of Jerusalem, 1970.

All cooking utensils which have been used for *hamez* in the course of the year are also forbidden for use on Passover, unless they have been cleansed according to *halakhic* requirements, since *hamez* has been absorbed into the walls of the vessels. This cleaning is called *kashering*. The method for *kashering,* utensils in which leaven has been cooked or boiled, is to immerse them in a cauldron of boiling water. Utensils that have been used with *hamez* on the open fire are *kashered* by heating them with fire until they glow. It is believed that the method in which food was absorbed into the utensils will also be effective in extracting it. However not all utensils can be treated in this way; earthenware utensils cannot be *kashered,* whereas glassware needs only to be soaked in water for three days with the water being changed every day. Many people have a complete set of utensils and crockery which are taken out and used on Passover, and put away immediately after the festival until the following year.

As yet we have only touched on the prohibition of eating *hamez* on Passover. However, Scripture states: "seven days no leaven shall be found in your houses," and "there shall not be seen with thee any leaven in all thy borders seven days." Thus no ḥameẓ at all is to remain in the possession of a Jew during Passover. The early rabbinic authorities also appended to this the prohibition that any ḥameẓ that has been in the possession of a Jew during Passover unwittingly, is forbidden even after Passover.

Consequently, traditional Jews attempt to ensure that every place to which ḥameẓ may have been brought is searched and cleaned. Here the Jewish woman comes into her own; although this is not specifically her job, she is the one who usually does it. The house is turned upside and inside out, clothes are searched and utensils scrubbed, in the attempt to remove all ḥameẓ before Passover starts. Fortunately the festival occurs in spring, and so coincides with the natural spring-cleaning instinct which many women seem to possess. This elaborate search is considered an absolute necessity; mere renunciation of one's ownership of all the ḥameẓ in one's possession was not considered sufficient. The reason for this, according to some rabbis, is that a man is by nature incapable of renouncing the ownership of his ḥameẓ with a full heart. Others held that even after such a renunciation, a man might find a piece of ḥameẓ in his house and, forgetting that it was Passover, eat it. The question to whom the ḥameẓ actually belonged would then be irrelevant, for it is forbidden to eat ḥameẓ, any ḥameẓ, on Passover. All ḥameẓ must therefore be searched out and removed before the festival.

All this searching and cleaning culminates on the night before Passover in a ceremony known as *bedikat ḥameẓ* (the search for

The Search

Detail from the *Golden Haggadah* showing the search for *Hameẓ* (leaven) by the light of a candle.

Detail from the *First Cincinnati Haggadah*, Germany, c.1480, showing a man using a feather to brush crumbs from a cupboard into a bowl as a part of the search for *ḥameẓ* (opposite).

hamez). After nightfall and the evening prayers and before any other activity is undertaken, the master of the house conducts a search through every corner of every room in which hamez may have been introduced during the preceding year. It is customary to make the search by the light of a candle which, according to the Talmud, is able to penetrate into even the darkest crannies. After a benediction of "the removal of hamez" has been recited, the search begins. All hamez that is found, with the exception of the food that is to be eaten that night and the following morning, is gathered up and put away in a safe place until morning when it will be burnt. It may well be that the womenfolk have cleaned the house so efficiently that no hamez at all is to be found. In order that the benediction should not be recited without reason, it has become the custom that members of the household, usually the children, place some small pieces of bread around the house in advance, taking care to remember how many pieces were placed, for if less were to be found, the whole house would have to be turned upside down again. Many follow the kabbalists of the Lurianic school who used to put out ten pieces, a number which represents the ten *Sefirot* or divine emanations.

When the ritual search has been completed, a declaration is recited in Aramaic, the vernacular of Talmud times, to the effect that all hamez that has been overlooked "should be like the dust of the earth."

The search for ḥameẓ in a Dutch household. Pen and wash drawing by Bernard Picart, 1725.

Some Jewish thinkers see ḥameẓ, that which rises and be- *As a Symbol*
comes leaven, as symbolically representing those tendencies in a
man which arouse him to evil. They see the whole process of
searching for the ḥameẓ and eliminating it as a reminder to man
that he should search through his deeds and purify his actions.
Mere renunciation of the imperfect past, one's own ḥameẓ, is not
sufficient; it must be destroyed. The pieces of ḥameẓ that are
placed around the house before the ritual search should then
remind a person of the fact that "there is not a person in the
world who does only good and never sins." And in the same way
that the ritual search for ḥameẓ always yields results, an examina-
tion of one's actions will always reveal room for improvement.
Life, however, should not consist of merely delving into the past,
so when a reasonable search has been completed, what has been

38

found will be rectified, and in this improved state the person will carry on until the process is repeated the following year.

Burning the Ḥamez

Ḥamez may be disposed of by means of any one of the four elements — fire, wind, water and dust. It may be burnt, or crumbled and scattered to the wind, or crushed and thrown to the sea, or ownership of it renounced by considering it void as the dust of the earth. However, the preferred method of disposal is burning. So on the morning of the eve of Passover, all the ḥamez that was found in the ritual search and the ḥamez which remains after breakfast is taken and burnt, an hour before midday. Originally it was to be disposed of before the time that the Paschal sacrifice could be brought to the Temple, which was at midday; from which time ḥamez could no longer be eaten. The rabbis decided to ensure this by setting the time for the prohibition against eating two hours earlier, and for the actual disposal one hour later. After burning it, another almost identical Aramaic formula is recited: "All leaven that is in my possession, that I may have seen or may not have seen, that I have destroyed or not destroyed, let it be nullified, and let it be ownerless as the dust of the earth." Both this and the preceding formula should be recited in a language that the householder understands.

The burning of ḥamez on Passover eve, Jerusalem.

The destruction of all *hamez* is obviously a great hardship for Sale
those who have large amounts of it, such as the owners of whiskey factories or bakeries. Thus the custom developed of selling
the *hamez* to a non-Jew. *Hamez* is sold before Passover nowadays
by means of a contract which to many seems to be a legal fiction.
An investigation of the four principal stages through which the
current method evolved, throws interesting light on Jewish
economic development. Originally whatever *hamez* was left over
before Passover was sold in the market place. Then, as Jews
became more involved with commerce and accumulated large
amounts of *hamez*, sales took place in which there was an under-
standing that the goods could be bought back. The goods were
still physically transferred to the premises of the purchaser for
the duration of the sale. The noted commentator on the Shulhan
Arukh, Rabbi Joel Sirkes (1541-1640), suggested that much in-
convenience could be avoided by leasing the rooms in which the
hamez was stored to the purchaser, and just handing over the
key. In order to ensure that it would be known that a sale had
actually taken place even though the goods were still on the
premises, the legal character of the sale was stressed and con-
tracts were written and signed. Later, as Jews came to live in
more closed communities, it was suggested that in order to ob-
viate the need for each individual to find a non-Jew to whom to
sell the *hamez*, a number of Jews should appoint an agent with a
power of attorney to act on their behalf to sell all their *hamez*
together.

Thus the custom nowadays is that an agent is appointed,
usually the local rabbi, and a document signed that gives him the
power of attorney to sell the *hamez* of the principals and lease
the places in which it is stored. The agent then draws up a legal
bill of sale, in full accordance with the *halakhah*. The sale will
then be completed by the signing of this contract, and by a
transfer of a small amount of money by a non-Jew in the form of
a down payment, which will of course be returned after Passover
when the property is bought back.

In Israel today, after having secured the signatures, through local rabbis, of all those who wish him to act as an agent on their behalf, the Chief Rabbi draws up a bill of sale, and on the morning before Passover sells their *ḥamez* to a non-Jew who may very well be a local Arab. A year or two ago, the Arab who was to buy all the *ḥamez* of Israel arrived a little later than the time arranged, which caused some worried faces, for had the *ḥamez* not been sold on time, most of the *ḥamez* in the State of Israel would have become forbidden to Jews for ever.

Mazzah

Mazzah is the only type of bread that may be eaten on Passover, and in fact all adult Jews are required to eat a piece of it on the first night of the festival. *Mazzah* is the antithesis of *ḥamez*; only grains that are capable of fermentation are valid for the making of *mazzah*. In practice, only wheat is used. Great care has to be taken to ensure that under no circumstances does the flour begin fermenting before baking.

There are three categories of flour which may be used for making *mazzah*, varying with the degree of supervision that the flour has undergone to ensure that it does not ferment. *Three Categories*

Mazzah shemurah, guarded *mazzah*, is made from flour that has been supervised from the time that the grain was harvested to

Inspection of hand baked *Mazzah shemurah*, Passover, 1953.

41

An 18th century etching of preparations for Passover. In the center is shown the baking of *Mazzah* and top left the cleaning of utensils. Top right, a man searches for *ḥameẓ* and directly below, the *ḥameẓ* is burnt.

ensure that it has not come into contact with water. Many people try to obtain this type of *mazzah* for fulfilling the religious duty of eating *mazzah* at the *seder* service on the first night of the festival, and some people eat only this kind for the whole of Passover.

The second category, known as Passover flour, is supervised from the time that the wheat was milled. This is the flour that is most commonly used on Passover.

The third category consists of flour for which there has been no special supervison for Passover, but is assumed not to have become fermented. This is used only in times of emergency.

42

The only ingredients that are used in *mazzah* are flour and water; not even salt is added. *Mazzah* is "the bread of poverty," of simplicity. Poor people have no choice but to adhere to essentials. They do not have time to wait for their bread to rise and become leaven, but when they are hungry and have the food, they prepare it and eat it immediately.

The Mishnah explains that *mazzah* is eaten to commemorate the haste with which the Israelites left Egypt, basing this on a verse in the Book of Exodus: "And they baked unleavened cakes of the dough which they brought forth out of Egypt, for it was not leavened; because they were thrust out of Egypt, and could not tarry, neither had they prepared for themselves victuals." Later commentators rejected the idea that history is merely an incidence of accidental happenings, and emphasized the fact that *mazzah*, made of only the basic ingredients, symbolizes purity and simplicity.

Mazzah made of flour mixed with wine, oil, milk, honey or eggs is known as *mazzah ashirah* ("rich *mazzah*"), and if no water is used it will be considered unleavened bread, though not suitable for the *seder* since the "bread of poverty" is specified. In strictly Orthodox circles, this *mazzah* is permitted during the remaining days of the festival only under special circumstances, such as for the sick and the aged.

When the *mazzah* is being baked, care is taken to ensure that the whole process from kneading to baking should not take longer than 18 minutes. However, there are factors that can accelerate or delay the process of fermentation. The flour and water are manipulated constantly, and since hot water accelerates the process of fermentation, it is customary to use "water which has rested overnight." It was believed that the water in wells became hot as the earth increased its heat during the night, so water was drawn in the evening and then left to rest overnight to cool. Nowadays in Jerusalem a festive procession can be seen on an evening before Passover winding its way to the Siloam spring on the outskirts of the Old City, from which water will be drawn and then left to rest overnight before being used for the baking of the *mazzot*.

The *mazzah* is usually perforated to allow the escape of air and thus retard the fermentation.

The introduction of machines in the middle of the 19th cen- *Machines* tury for milling the flour and then for baking the *mazzah*, sparked off a heated controversy, echoes of which can still be heard today. The argument centered on two problems. Did the milling cause the wheat to exude moisture which would bring about

The preparation and baking of *mazzot,* in a 17th century Dutch woodcut.

fermentation? And secondly, although once *mazzah* has been fully baked it cannot become fermented, did the pieces of dough which adhered to the machinery before they were fully baked, become fermented? Pamphlets were distributed by both sides. The opinion that prevailed was that all depended on the type of machines used, and also on the supervision of the process. The use of machines for *mazzah* is now widespread. Some see it as preferable to handbaked *mazzah* since the unevenness of hand-baked *mazzah* makes for the possibility that some of the flour may remain unbaked and subsequent contact with water would cause it to ferment and become *hamez*.

44

However, there are still some who insist on baking their own *mazzah*, not only because of the halakhic objections mentioned above, but also for the extra merit of performing the *mitzvah* oneself, despite the machine age in which we live.

In apprehension of fermentation even after baking, some Hasidim refrain throughout Passover from eating any *mazzah* or *mazzah* meal that has been soaked in water, known in Yiddish as *"gebrokt."* This means that they forgo the pleasure of eating dumplings made of *mazzah* meal which are known as *kneidlach,* a

Mazzah piercers from either southern Germany or Alsace, 19th cent.

very popular Passover dish among Ashkenazim. There is, however, a tendency to be lenient on the eighth day that is added in the Diaspora.

The obligation to eat *mazzah* on the first night is stated in the Torah. Great efforts have always been made to ensure that *mazzah* be available for all, and even the rigors of life under the Soviet regime have not prevented Jews from fulfilling this obligation. Supplies of *mazzah* produced in underground bakeries have been supplemented by smuggling and by shipments from Western Jewry. There is no obligation to eat *mazzah* on any of the remainng days of Passover, though some rabbis were of the opinion

45

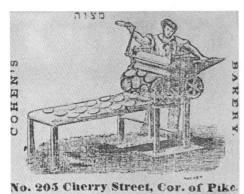

מצה

COHEN'S BAKERY

No. 205 Cherry Street, Cor. of Pike.
ENTRANCE IN PIKE STREET.

Advertisement for *mazzah*, showing an early *mazzah* machine. New York, 1855 (left).

Mazzah dough being perforated and cut before going into the oven at a Bene-Berak, Israel factory (opposite left).

Mazzah on conveyor belt coming out of oven. (opposite right).

that the eating of *mazzah* during these remaining days also constitutes a *mitzvah* (religious precept). It is told that the Gaon of Vilna was in the habit of eating additional meals during Passover in order to perform this extra *mitzvah*.

The Benediction

The usual benediction for bread ending with the words "Who bringest forth bread from the earth" is also recited for *mazzah*, but at the *seder* an additional benediction "over the eating of *mazzah*" is also recited. The minimum amount that is to be eaten at the *seder* is the technical equivalent of an olive's bulk, which is approximately two thirds of a machine-made *mazzah* of regular size. In order to appreciate the taste of this *mazzah*, some traditional Jews do not eat any *mazzah* for the whole preceding month starting from the festival of Purim, while others refrain from the beginning of the month of Nisan. According to the Talmud one must abstain from eating *mazzah* at least for the day before the *seder*: "Whoever eats *mazzah* on the day before Passover is to be compared to a man who makes love to his fiancée in his father-in-law's house."

The Fast of the Firstborn
The Talmud recounts that Rabbi Judah ha-Nasi, the compiler of the Mishnah, would abstain from all food on the day before

Passover so as to have an appetite for the *mazzah* and the *seder* meal. Already in the time of the Mishnah a fast was observed on this day by all firstborn males as a way of showing their gratitude to God for having spared the Jewish firstborn when their Egyptian counterparts were smitten in the tenth plague. This fast is to be observed by all males who are firstborn either to their mother or father. If the child is too young, his father fasts for him, but if the father is himself a firstborn, the child's mother fasts for him. If the day before Passover should happen to be a Saturday, the fast will then be brought forward to the preceding Thursday. However, the fast may be completely suspended for a *seudat mitzvah*, a meal that is eaten in connection with the fulfillment of a *mitzvah*.

The completion (*siyyum* in Hebrew) of the study of a trac- *The Siyyum* tate of Talmud always constitutes a sufficient reason for such a celebrative meal. Consequently the custom has evolved that a tractate is finished in the synagogue on the morning of the eve of Passover, and all the firstborn of the neighborhood crowd in and listen to the final lines of the tractate being read and explained by the rabbi, or by whoever it is that so conveniently completes a tractate on this day. All those present then participate in the meal of celebration for this event and are thus relieved of the

47

duty of fasting. Consequently the "fast of the firstborn" is to all intents and purposes not observed.

The day before Passover is thus spent in disposing of the last of the *hamez* and burning it, and then preparing for the *seder*, the highlight of the Passover celebrations.

4. BECAUSE OF WHAT THE LORD DID FOR ME

"God made man because He loves stories," Rabbi Nahaman of Bratslav is reputed to have said. Men certainly love stories, and on the first night of Passover Jews around the world congregate with their families or in other groups to celebrate the *seder*, the central activity of which is the recounting of the going out of Egypt. The Exodus is mentioned in the prayers every single day of the year, but on the first night of Passover (two nights in the Diaspora) it is not sufficient just to mention the Exodus. The story must be told, and thus shared with others. That is done with the aid of audio-visual techniques which, although centuries old, would be appreciated by the most modern educationalists: *mazzah* and bitter herbs are eaten, four cups of wine are drunk, and the participants eat while reclining, instead of sitting as usual.

Reclining

Reclining was prescribed for certain parts of the ceremony because in the ancient, particularly the Roman, world it was the way of free people. This custom is mentioned in the Mishnah. On this night every Jew, rich or poor, is free and noble and acts it out by reclining; the left side is recommended so as to avoid

Reclining at the Passover *seder*, illustrated in the *Bird's Head Haggadah*, Germany, c. 1300. The human figures have birds' heads to comply with the commandment forbidding graven images.

48

"The Passover Meal" by Moritz Oppenheim, with the head of the family wearing the traditional *kitel*. Germany, c. 1860.

discomfort whilst eating. Reclining is obligatory for the drinking of the four cups of wine, for the eating of the first piece of *mazzah*, Hillel's sandwich and the *afikoman*. Some rabbis are of the opinion that in modern times reclining no longer conveys the feeling of freedom, and the practice of reclining is therefore not widespread today. The narration of the story is interspersed with many unfamiliar actions that are intended to fill the participants, especially the children, with amazement and curiosity, in the hope that they *will* be stimulated into asking for an explanation. Their questions will provide the cue for the unfolding of the story of the liberation from Egypt. "And it shall come to pass when your son shall ask you: 'What means this service to you? ' . . . And you shall tell your son on that day: 'Because of what the Lord did for me when I went out of Egypt.'"

The rituals of the *seder* are not just gimmicks: they are also symbols of events in Jewish history, and many of them also embody values that are relevant for the present and the future. Before discussing the narration, we will first consider the ritual of the *seder*.

Seder

The word *seder* denotes the clearly-defined order of the ceremonial service of this first night of Passover. It commences soon after nightfall with the chanting of the opening lines of the *Haggadah*. It may not be started earlier, for the story must be told "when *mazzah* and bitter herbs are in front of you" — and that is at night. It should not be delayed long after nightfall so that children will be able to stay awake, and also so that the *afikoman*, which is eaten at the end of the meal, will be eaten before midnight.

The *seder* is usually conducted by a leader or master of ceremonies, who sometimes wears a white robe as a symbol of purity and rejoicing. In family groups, the head of the family will usually perform this function, and at a communal *seder* it may well be the communal rabbi. In many rites it is the custom for one of the

Master of Ceremonies

50

participants to intone the appropriate descriptive phrase before each part of the ceremony.

The Order
In some rites these phrases are chanted as a separate litany.

KADDESH   A benediction over a goblet of wine, sanctifying the day.

REHAZ   Wash the hands without reciting a benediction.

KARPAS   Dip a vegetable, such as potato, radish, celery or parsley, into some salt water, and eat it.

YAHAZ   Break the middle *mazzah,* and hide half of it for the *afikoman.*

MAGGID   Tell the story, and sing praises to the Lord over the second cup of wine, which will be drunk at the end of this part.

RAHZAH   Wash the hands before the meal, with a benediction.

MOZI MAZZAH   Recite the usual benediction for bread, and the additional benediction for *mazzah;* eat a piece of the upper *mazzah* and of the remaining part of the middle *mazzah.*

MAROR   Eat bitter herbs dipped in *haroset.*

KOREKH   Eat a sandwich of the bottom *mazzah* and bitter herbs dipped in *haroset.*

SHULHAN OREKH   The festive meal.

ZAFUN   Eat the hidden piece of the middle *mazzah,* the *afikoman.*

BAREKH   Grace after Meals over the third cup of wine.

HALLEL   Sing further songs of praise, after which the fourth cup of wine is drunk.

NIRZAH   "Acceptance" — God has found the actions performed acceptable, and appropriate hymns are recited.

Detail from the *Erlangen Haggadah* showing miniature illustrations of each section of the *seder* service. Germany, 1747.

Detail from the 14th century *Barcelona Haggadah* with the initial letters representing the order of the *seder* service.

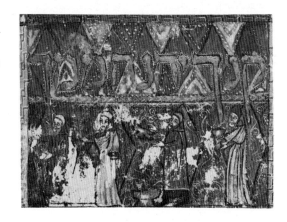

Seder Plate

Many of the objects that are used in the course of the ceremony are arranged on a *seder*-plate, which may well be a plate that has been specially made for use at the *seder*.

Opinions vary as to the objects that are to be placed on this plate, and as to their arrangement. Most people follow the arrangement of the kabbalist, Rabbi Isaac Luria of Safed, known as the Ari, who set out the objects to correspond to the ten *Sefirot* or divine emanations, which are named in brackets under the names of the objects in the first diagram.

Each of these objects has a story to tell.

Three Mazzot

Three whole *mazzot* are placed on the *seder*-plate. Two of these are needed for the benediction over bread. On all Sabbaths and festivals, each meal opens with a benediciton made over two whole loaves of bread, which represent the Manna that miraculously fell in the parched wilderness and fed the Children of Israel during their forty years of wanderings. On the Sabbath day it was forbidden to gather Manna, but two portions fell the day before, hence the two loaves.

The extra *mazzah*, the middle one, commemorates the Exodus from Egypt and is the "bread of poverty." Early in the

52

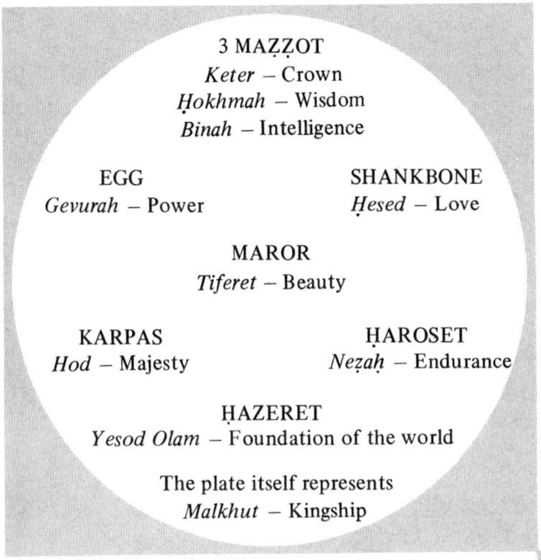

THE ARI

3 MAZZOT
Keter – Crown
Hokhmah – Wisdom
Binah – Intelligence

EGG
Gevurah – Power

SHANKBONE
Hesed – Love

MAROR
Tiferet – Beauty

KARPAS
Hod – Majesty

HAROSET
Nezah – Endurance

HAZERET
Yesod Olam – Foundation of the world

The plate itself represents
Malkhut – Kingship

THE GAON OF VILNA

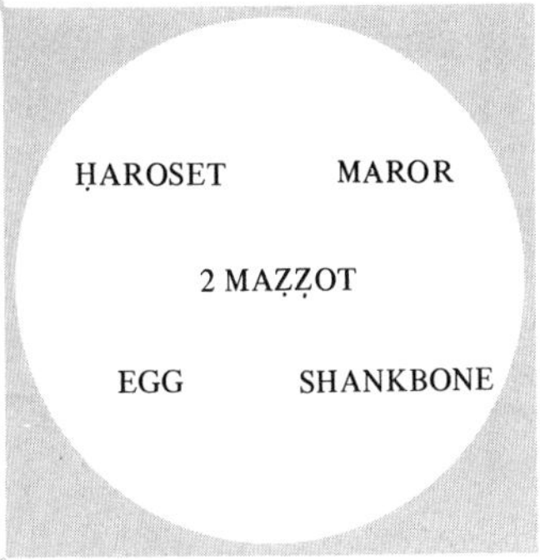

HAROSET   MAROR

2 MAZZOT

EGG   SHANKBONE

OTHERS

EGG   SHANKBONE

3 MAZZOT

HAROSET   MAROR

Seder – Plate Arrangements

53

service it is broken in two, for poor people are accustomed to break their bread and share it. Another and less romantic explanation is that the poor usually break off one piece of their bread, putting away the other piece for the next meal. Be that as it may, half of this middle *mazzah* is hidden away to be used for the *afikoman*, and the other half is used for the special benediction over *mazzah* just before the meal starts.

The procedure will then be as follows. The first blessing, the *mozi*, is said whilst holding the two whole *mazzot* with the piece of "poor man's bread" in the middle. The bottom *mazzah* is then laid on the table, and the second benediction "over the eating of *mazzah*" is said whilst holding the upper *mazzah* and the middle piece. A piece of the upper *mazzah* and the middle broken one is then eaten. The bottom *mazzah* will be used later for *korekh* (Hillel's sandwich).

Afikoman

The broken piece of *mazzah* that was hidden away early in the ceremony is known as the *afikoman*. This word may be connected with a Greek term meaning something to do with after-meal entertainment or dessert. The Mishnah which states that "one may not add *afikoman* after the Passover meal" is usually interpreted to mean that no dessert may be eaten after the Passover meal: it is to be the last food eaten. When the Temple was destroyed and the Paschal sacrifice was no longer brought, the piece of *mazzah* known as the *afikoman*, which is eaten as a symbolic reminder of that sacrifice, also came to be eaten at the end of the meal so that no food should follow it, but the taste should linger. Care is also taken to eat the *afikoman* before midnight, as was required of the Paschal sacrifice.

Among Ashkenazi communities it has become the custom for *Stealing* children to attempt to "steal" the *afikoman* from its hiding place, and then demand a ransom for its return. This ruse encouraged children to stay awake for the reading of the Haggadah. The ransom could not be demanded until the end of the meal

54

Silver tiered *seder*-plate, Germany, 1802. There are four figures and an egg cup on the upper tray (left). Detail from the *Birds' Head Haggadah*, Germany, c. 1300, showing the hiding of the *afikoman* (right).

when the *afikoman* was needed, and by then the main part of the Haggadah, the story, had been read. This practice is quite unknown in Sephardi communities.

However it is the main among these communities that other fascinating *afikoman* customs grew. Among Baghdadi Jews the custom was for one of the participants to leave the room, disguise himself as a traveller, and tie the *afikoman* in a bundle on his back. When he re-entered the room the person leading the service would ask him:

> "Where are you from? "
> "Egypt," would be the reply.
> "And where are you going? "
> "To Jerusalem! "

To Jerusalem

55

It is worth noting that in 1949 when the government of Iraq gave all Jews who wished a period of six months in which to leave the country, out of the 125,000-strong Jewish community in Iraq, whose history can be traced back for over 2,000 years, 120,000 Jews seized their opportunity and eventually arrived in Jerusalem in a dramatic airlift known as operation "Ali Baba."

The Jews of Djerba have another delightful custom. It is said *The End* that there have been Jews on the island of Djerba, off the coast *of Exile* of Tunisia, ever since the destruction of the first Temple in 586 b.c.e. When the Jews were exiled, a group of them took a stone of their precious sanctuary with them as a sacred relic and this stone miraculously grew larger and larger. When they could no longer carry it they stopped and built their synagogue over it in Hara Kabira, until recently one of the two villages in the island inhabited only by Jews. However, they never forgot that they were in exile. And on Passover night the one conducting the *seder* would give the *afikoman* to one of the family, who would go out and visit relatives and neighbors with it, and forecast for them all that the Messiah was coming. The majority of the Jews of Djerba ended their exile only recently when they immigrated to the new State of Israel.

Among Kurdish Jews it was the custom to tie the *afikoman* on to the arm of a growing son, and say: "May you so tie the *Ketubbah* (the marriage document) to the arm of your bride! "

In folkloristic belief the *afikoman* has been endowed with a *Folklore* special sanctity that lasts even after Passover. A piece of it was

Interior of the Ghariba synagogue, Hara al-Saghira, Djerba.

56

kept throughout the year as a protection against the "evil eye," or as an aid to longevity. In such places as Iran, Afghanistan, Bukhara, Kurdistan, and also Salonika, many Jews kept a piece of the *afikoman* in their pockets or in their houses throughout the year for good luck. In some places, pregnant women would carry a piece of the *afikoman* around together with salt and coral stones for protection, and would hold it in their hand during delivery. There was even a belief that it was effective against fire, and a piece of *afikoman* kept for seven years could stop the seas flooding; it was after all on the "Feast of Unleavened Bread" that the waters of the Red Sea parted for the Children of Israel. Many folk stories are told of the powers of the *afikoman,* but we must return to the explanation of the *seder*-plate.

Shankbone

The shankbone (*zero'a* in Hebrew) on the *seder*-plate commemorates the roasted Paschal sacrifice that can no longer be offered; the bone is usually roasted or boiled. The *zero'a* (which literally means forearm) of the animal was selected because it gives the opportunity to tell the story of how it was "with an outstretched arm" that He brought us out of Egypt.

Egg

The roasted egg on the *seder*-plate commemorates the roasted *ḥagigah,* the sacrifice that in Temple times was offered on each festival. In many communities it is the custom to eat this egg at the beginning of the meal, dipped in salt water.

One reason an egg is used for this purpose is its roundness. Symbolizing the life cycle, it was used as a symbol of mourning; it is eaten by mourners on their return from the funeral, and also at the last meal before the fast of the 9th of Av that commemorates the destruction of the two Temples. Thus Rabbi Moses Isserles, in his authoritative notes on the Shulhan Arukh, writes that the egg at the *seder* commemorates the destruction of the Temple, after which the Paschal sacrifice was discontinued. In-

Seder in a Joint Distribution Committee children's home in Budapest, 1948. The children are about to eat the egg in salt water.

deed, a note of sobriety is introduced for this reason into all Jewish celebrations. The glass which is broken at a wedding ceremony is likewise a reminder of the destruction of the Temple. Thus, despite the fact that the *seder* is a legitimately joyful celebration of the Exodus from Egypt, an egg is put on the *seder*-plate to introduce some seriousness into the proceedings.

A more homiletical reason is that the Jewish people are like the egg. Unlike other foods, the more an egg is cooked the harder it becomes. Similarly, the more they are persecuted the tougher the Jews become. The Bible records in connection with the slavery in Egypt: "But the more they afflicted them, the more they multiplied and the more they spread abroad." The harsh and bitter years of slavery and subjection were to mold a tribe of individuals into a nation with a common history of suffering, united in their aspirations: "This year we are here, next year in the land of Israel; this year we are slaves, next year free men! "

Bitter Herbs

The bitterness of past suffering is nevertheless remembered: *maror* (a bitter herb) is eaten at the *seder*. The herbs that were considered suitable for the *seder* are those plants whose common characteristics are "bitterness, possessing sap, with a graying appearance." *Ḥazeret* (lettuce) is often used, as is horseradish,

58

Detail from the *Joel ben Shimon Haggadah,* showing a man holding the bitter herbs.

known in **Yiddish** as *khrein*; some use both. After the benediction, ending with the words "over the eating of *maror,*" an amount which is the technical equivalent of an olive's bulk is eaten by each of the participants, seated in an upright position for this part of the ceremony.

The Mishnah states that the bitter herbs commemorate the condition of the Israelites in Egypt: "Because the Egyptians made the lives of our forefathers bitter in Egypt, as it is said: 'And they made their lives bitter with hard service, in mortar and bricks, and in all kinds of work in the field; in all their work they made them serve with rigor.' "

Is there a purpose in remembering past bitterness? Rabbi A.I. Kook felt that the ability to feel bitterness when exploited by others indicates that one's mind and emotions have not yet become completely enslaved; in fact it is these feelings that impel a man to self-liberation. The bitter herbs that are eaten at the *seder* table should remind a person of the existence of bitterness in the past, enable him to distinguish between bitter and sweet in the present, and fortify him for the challenges that are to be overcome in the future.

Korekh

Hillel the Elder (first century c.e.) would not eat the bitter herbs on their own. For him the verse "On unleavened bread and bitter herbs shall they eat it," referring to the Paschal sacrifice, implied that they should be eaten together. He would therefore make a sandwich (*korekh*) of the Passover sacrifice and *mazzah* and *maror* — according to some versions just *mazzah* and *maror* — and eat them together. It has become the custom in all rites nowadays that after a piece of *maror* has been eaten on its own, another piece is taken and made into a sandwich with the lowest of the three *mazzot*, and an explanatory formula is recited, beginning with the words, "In memory of the Temple according to Hillel."

Haroset

Before one eats the bitter herbs as well as the sandwich made with them, they are dipped into *haroset*, a paste made of fruit, spices, wine and *mazzah* meal. The word *haroset* may be connected with *heres*, clay, which it is supposed to resemble in color, and symbolizes the mortar that the Jews made in Egypt. The specific ingredients vary. Ashkenazim make it from apples, chopped almonds, cinnamon and red wine. In some Sephardi communities attempts are made to use the seven fruits of the Holy Land mentioned in the Bible. North Africans add some rather pungent spices to their mixture, and Yementies use chili pepper.

Karpas

On the *seder*-plate, according to the arrangement of the Ari, there is some *karpas*; the etymological derivation of this word is obscure. Vegetables such as potatoes, radishes, celery or parsley are used for this. Near the beginning of the ceremony, a small amount of this vegetable, less than the equivalent of an olive's bulk, is dipped in salt water and eaten by each of the participants. This action may be counted upon to arouse the interest of the children present, and indeed even of the older people, for after eating this appetizer people forget about their food, and start telling stories.

60

Salt Water

There is a bowl of salt-water on the table, in some rites on the *seder*-plate, to represent the tears that the Israelites shed in Egypt. It is used for dipping the *karpas*, and also for the egg by those who are accustomed to commencing the meal proper by eating the egg dipped in salt water, which is the custom in many communities.

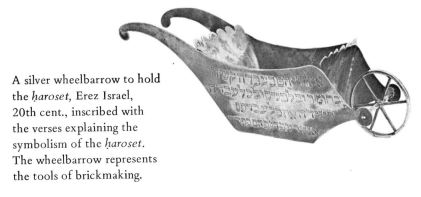

A silver wheelbarrow to hold the *haroset*, Erez Israel, 20th cent., inscribed with the verses explaining the symbolism of the *haroset*. The wheelbarrow represents the tools of brickmaking.

The Meal

The food at the meal is usually festive, although no specific menu is recommended. Sephardim and North African Jews generally eat lamb as the main course, and amongst Ashkenazim *kneidlach* (dumplings made of *mazzah* meal) are a common dish. The meal is enjoyed in a festive and jolly atmosphere, songs are sung, and if wine is taken it does not count in the reckoning of the four cups.

The Four Cups

On the table there will also be quite a few bottles or decanters of wine. The rabbis enjoined that men and women alike are each to drink *arba kosot* (four cups) of wine during the seder: "A man is duty bound to sell his clothes, or to borrow money, or to hire himself out to obtain wine for the four cups." The Mishnah states that the poor must also drink four cups of wine, even if it

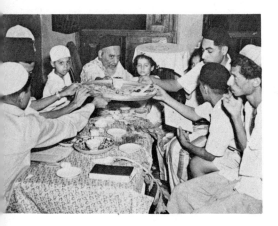 

has to be provided by charity funds. People should drink the four
cups even at the risk of becoming intoxicated. The story is told
in the Talmud that Rabbi Judah son of Ilai, whose face it seems
was always red and shining, was accused by a noble Roman lady
of being "a teacher and a drunkard." He replied: "Believe me, I
taste [no wine] but that of *Kiddush* and *Havdalah* and the four
cups of Passover, on account of which I have to bind my temples
from Passover to Shavu'ot."

Red wine should be drunk because of its quality. In the *Red Wine*
Middle Ages, the blood libel brought about the use of white wine
— a precaution that did not always help.

The amount to be drunk for each cup is at least a quarter of a
log (0.137 liter). One's duty has not been performed if they are
all drunk at once: they are to be drunk in order at specified parts
of the service. The first cup is drunk for *Kiddush*, the sanctification, the second at the conclusion of the main part of the
Haggadah, the third after Grace after Meals, while the fourth is
drunk after the recitation of *Nishmat*. It is the usual Sabbath and
Festival custom to use a cup of wine for Kiddush and, in some
rites, for Grace after meals, so in effect only two cups are added.
However, whereas normally it is sufficient for the person con-

62

Seder in Aden, 1949. The *seder* plate is being raised by all the participants (opposite left).

Children at the seder, perhaps planning how to steal the *afikoman*. Note the simple *seder*-plate in the center of the table (opposite right).

Yemenite *seder* in Israel. Note the various bitter herbs on the table.

ducting a service to drink these cups, at the *seder* all the participants are obligated to drink all four cups.

Many reasons are given for the fact that the number of cups *Four* to be drunk is four. Four is a common number generally in Jewish ritual. There are four *zizit*, fringes worn on the corners of the *talit;* there are four portions of the Torah in the phylacteries, four kinds of plants are taken and waved on Sukkot (the Festival of Tabernacles). On Passover four is an especially popular number; there are four questions, four sons mentioned in the *Haggadah*, four pieces of *mazzah* (two whole and two halves). Some see these four cups as corresponding to the four kingdoms that are mentioned in the Book of Daniel as having oppressed Israel —

Bukharan *seder* in Israel.

63

the Chaldeans, the Medes, and the Romans whom God will ultimately requite with four cups of retribution. Alternatively, they correspond to the four cups of consolation which God will give Israel to drink. The accepted explanation is that these four cups symbolize the four expressions of redemption that are found in the Book of Exodus: "I will bring you out ... I will deliver you ... I will redeem you ... I will take you to me for a people." However, there is also a fifth expression there: "I will bring you in unto the land ... " According to some manuscripts of the Babylonian Talmud, Rabbi Tarfon was of the opinion that a fifth cup should also be drunk. This was also the opinion of many of the *geonim,* and in Yemenite communities five cups are drunk. This optional cup is drunk between the third and fourth cups at the end of *Hallel.*

The Cup of Elijah

The majority, who drink only four cups, fill an extra cup of wine between the third and fourth cups, just after the Grace after Meals. However, this cup is not for the participants: it will be left on the table. This is known as the cup of Elijah. The prophet Elijah, who according to tradition never died, is considered to be the harbinger of the coming of the Messiah, who will relieve Jews of all their suffering. The cup is filled and Elijah welcomed at this point of the ceremony, because it is at this juncture in the *seder* that the doors can at last be opened. They should have been open all the time, for this is a "night of watching" in which God protects all Jews. Furthermore, an invitation was issued at the beginning of the *seder*: "Let all who are hungary come and eat, let all who have need come and celebrate the Passover! " – and

Detail from 15th century *First Nuremberg Haggadah* showing the drinking of the second of the four cups of wine.

64

The Messiah wearing a medieval Jewish hat, riding a white donkey, being led into Jerusalem by the prophet, Elijah. From a *Haggadah,* Munich, 15th cent.

Glass cup of Elijah. Vienna (?), c. 1800 (left).

how could they come if the doors were not open? However, the blood libel made the *seder* night a dangerous occasion for Jews, and hence doors would be locked against attacks. After the meal, nevertheless, the doors would be briefly opened so that all should remember that this was a "night of watching." Many tales are told of the eager expectancy with which the participants at the *seder* ceremony have awaited the coming of Elijah. Children closely watch the cup of Elijah to see if the level has miraculously gone down. After the cup of Elijah is filled, Elijah is invited to come and bring devastation on those who have "made Thy abodes desolate." For "just as the Almighty redeemed us from Egypt, so will he redeem us again and send us Elijah the prophet to bring us the good tidings."

5. AND YOU SHALL TELL YOUR SON

A Talk-Feast

Haggadah means narration, and it is the name given to the text used for the narrating of the story of the Exodus which is the

65

core of the *seder* ceremony. The narration was ordained in the Torah, and in the days when the Paschal sacrifice formed the central part of the celebrations, the story was told at the Paschal meal. After the Second Temple was destroyed, the narration of the story at the *seder* became the central activity of the night: the *seder* became a talk-feast. The Greeks and the Romans used to hold symposia and dialogues at banquets where they would recline in a leisurely manner on cushions, and imbibe large quantities of wine, all the while talking and debating. It is possible that the form of these banquets may have affected the form of the *seder* ceremony. However, parts of the text of the *Haggadah* are very old and were compiled before the times of the Greeks and the Romans. Much of the text appears in the Mishnah, additions were made to this, and it was apparently compiled as a separate book in the eighth century c.e. by one of the *geonim*. The *Haggadah* was not written by any particular author or group of authors, and so it is not a "literary composition" in the accepted sense of the term. It is rather a collection of narrative sources interspersed with ritual, with added songs of thanksgiving and joy.

The narrative itself which is composed of excerpts from the Bible, Mishnah and Midrash, is not very long and occupies only a part of the *Haggadah*. It is intended to serve as the basis for discussion of past history and future aspirations, for there are no

The More One Tells

The *seder*, from a 14th cent. Spanish *Haggadah*.

limits as to how much discussion is to take place. The *Haggadah* states at the outset: "The more one tells of the story of the Exodus, the more praiseworthy it is." In some places, prolonged discussion on the *Haggadah* causes the *seder* ceremony to extend for hours. As they tell the story of how their ancestors were liberated from slavery in Egypt, it is likely that many Jews will recall their own personal escapes from similar, if not worse, situations. In fact a Mishnah is quoted in the *Haggadah* to prove that the Exodus is not to be narrated merely as a record of historical fact, but also as being within the realm of personal experience: "In every generation a man is duty-bound to regard himself as if he went out from Egypt." Thus songs of praise are sung to God, "Who raiseth up the poor out of the dust, And lifteth up the needy out of the dunghill." And if those present have not yet managed to escape, their hopes might be revitalized by the lessons of history: "This year we are slaves, next year free men." In this vein, the psalms of praise are followed by a prayer for the future redemption.

We will now consider the various parts of the *Haggadah* as they unfold in the *seder* ceremony.

Kiddush

The ceremony opens with the chanting of *kiddush* (the sanctification), over a cup of wine, as is the custom on Sabbaths and festivals. The benediction over wine is said first, and then one sanctifying the day. This is the same text as that chanted on the other two pilgrim festivals, except for the reference to Passover, "the season of our liberation." This is followed by the blessing "who has kept us alive and maintained us and enabled us to reach this season." If the *seder* should take place on a Saturday night, this last blessing is preceded by two additional blessings that mark the exit of the Sabbath.

The Invitation

The Haggadah itself starts with a passage in Aramaic, full of

Copperplate engraving by Bernard Picart of the *seder* meal as celebrated by Portuguese Jews in Amsterdam, 1723.

promise and hope: "This is the bread of affliction that our fathers did eat in the land of Egypt! " — yet they were redeemed. And although this year we are here, "next year in Jerusalem; this year we are slaves, next year free men." This passage is recited at the beginning of the ceremony to emphasize to all those participating that whatever their situation may be, they will be redeemed, just as were their ancestors. However, in the middle of this passage an invitation is extended: "Let all who are poor come and eat, let all who are in need come and make the Passover! " One might expect that after such an invitation the meal would be started; it is not. In fact in some communities the whole table is now removed from the room as if the meal were over. This is done to perplex the children. It is also at this juncture that the second cup of wine is filled, which is also confusing, since it is not customary to drink more than one cup before a meal.

Four Questions

If questions have not yet been asked, the *Haggadah* ensures that they will be, and four prepared questions follow: "Why is this night different from all other nights? (or, more correctly, "How different is this night from all other nights! "

1. For on all other night we may eat *hamez* and *mazzah*: on this night only *mazzah*.
2. For on all other nights we may eat all kinds of vegetables: on this night we must eat bitter herbs.
3. For on all other nights we do not dip (our vegetables) even once: on this night we dip twice (the *karpas* into salt water, and the bitter herbs into *haroset*).
4. For on all other nights we may eat either sitting up straight or reclining: on this night we all recline."

The first three of these questions appear in the Mishnah. The fourth question there dwells on the fact that on this night the meat of the Paschal sacrifice must be roasted, and this was omitted after the destruction of the Temple. In order that the number of questions should remain four, the question on reclining was introduced.

In Mishnaic times the narration took place after the meal; hence it would have been noticed that "only *mazzah*" was eaten, or bitter herbs were eaten, or that dipping took place. When the rabbis decided that the *Haggadah* should be read before the meal to ensure that children should stay awake for it, the questions remained unchanged, and are usually taught to children in advance.

These four questions are popularly known as the *Mah Nish-* *Asked by* *tanah*, after the opening words in Hebrew, and they are asked by *the Young*

Kurdi *seder* in Jerusalem, 1970, with ritual raising of *seder*-plate (left).
Passover *seder* in a Jerusalem school, 1971. The children's parents are invited to watch what is in fact a rehearsal for the home ceremony (right).

one of the children of the family. If no child is able to do so, the wife asks them. If she cannot, a man must ask them himself: "Even two learned men who are well versed in the laws of Passover should ask each other questions." Nowadays it is the custom for the youngest present to ask them; often all the youngsters chant the four questions in unison.

An Italian faience *seder*-plate made in Padua in 1673. The text in the center of the plate is the *kiddush* for Passover followed by the order of the *seder*.

An initial-word panel from the 15th century *Joel ben Shimon Haggadah* with marginal illustrations of a Passover table (opposite).

A rather cynical modern Hebrew poet was of the opinion that there were far more important and relevant questions that should be asked on Passover. A *Haggadah* printed in 1938 in Kibbutz Ein Harod contains the following four questions:

Another Four Questions

1. Why is so much blood now being shed in the world?
2. Why do people all over the world hate Jews?
3. When will the people of Israel return to this land?
4. When will our country be a fertile and luxuriant garden?

Unfortunately, the answers are not contained in this kibbutz *Haggadah*.

70

הָא לַחְמָא עַנְיָא דִי אֲכָלוּ אַבְהָתָנָא
בְּאַרְעָא דְמִצְרָיִם כָּל דִכְפִין
יֵיתֵי וְיֵכֹל כָּל דִצְרִיךְ יֵיתֵי
וְיִפְסַח הַשַׁתָּא הָכָא לְשָׁנָה
הַבָּאָה בְּאַרְעָא דְיִשְׂרָאֵל הַשַׁתָּא

71

The Answer

The answer that is given to the *Mah Nishtanah* in the *Haggadah* is very simple: "We were slaves to Pharaoh in Egypt." If God had not delivered our ancestors "with a mighty hand and an out-stretched arm," we would still be slaves. That is why this night is different.

Great pains were taken to ensure that the story and its significance would be understood by all. The *Haggadah* was translated into the vernaculars used by Jews, and into the languages of many of the countries in which Jews found themselves, especially so that it should be easier for their womenfolk to understand. In Jewish law women are exempt from the positive *mitzvot* (precepts) that are to be performed at specific times. However, despite the fact that the *Haggadah* is to be recited at a specific time, women were also obliged to participate in the *mitzvah* of narrating the story, because they "also took part in the miracle." In fact, according to the Midrash it was the righteousness of the women of Israel that caused God to remember His people and liberate them. The standard of education for Jewish women through the ages was not always high, often intentionally so; thus many rabbis would translate every word of the *Haggadah* as they recited it so that the women present should also understand.

Hundreds of commentaries have been written on this small book for those desiring more intricate explanations of the details

Two pages from a kibbutz *Haggadah*, illustrated by Shmuel Katz. The text includes a non-traditional set of four questions.

72

Painted linen Passover banner, showing Adam and Eve in the Garden of Eden. The text above lists the component parts of the *seder* ceremony while that below lists the ten plagues. Germany, early 19th century.

Above: Ceramic *seder* dish depicting a family at *seder*. Hungary, early 19th century. Below: Majolica *seder* dish showing the position of the various items to be used. Czechoslovakia, 19th century.

Retelling the story of the Exodus around the *seder* table. Engraving from the 18th century *Erlangen Haggadah*.

and implications of the "going out of Egypt," for even knowledgeable and scholarly people who might know the whole Torah, were required to retell the story every year.

To illustrate this point, the *Haggadah* cites the story of five *Five Rabbis* of the foremost rabbis in Erez Israel during the period of Roman occupation in the first century after the destruction of the second Temple. They were reclining around the *seder* table in Bene-Berak, yet despite their vast knowledge they discussed the story of the going out of Egypt for the entire night. They only stopped when they were informed by their pupils: "Rabbis! The time has come for the reading of the morning prayer."

The Talmud records that Rabbi Akiva and other leading rab- *Revolt again* bis gave their full support to the Bar Kokhba revolt against the *the Romans* Roman occupation of Erez Israel in 135 c.e. Some scholars are of the opinion that the *seder* mentioned here in the *Haggadah* was taking place in a cave where the rabbis were hiding from the Romans at the time of that revolt. There must have been some reason that these rabbis did not celebrate the *seder* with their families. The assumption that they were in a cave is based on the fact that there were no windows, since they had to be informed that day was breaking by their students, who may have been on guard outside the cave. It may well be that the story of the liberation from Egypt that they were so avidly discussing, inspired them in their bid for liberation from the Romans. It was also on Passover, nearly 2,000 years later, that the fighters of the Warsaw Ghetto were to make their desperate stand against the Nazis. Their inspiration came from the same source.

73

There are many different levels on which the story can be told. To demonstrate this the *Haggadah* extracts four passages from the Pentateuch, and explains them as four different questions that four types of sons ask, and the four diverse answers they receive. A wise son, a wicked one, a simple son, and a son who cannot ask questions, are all identified from the content of these questions and answers that appear in the Pentateuch. Many commentators give lengthy explanations of the significance of the division of the sons into these four types, as well as the different educational methods that are necessary for answering different types of sons.

The various ways in which the four sons have been depicted in illustrated *Haggadot* provide a commentary on changing attitudes. The wise son is often drawn with a long beard, poring over books. The wicked son is depicted in various poses; in some editions he is a soldier, in others a boxer, in others a cleanshaven hatless businessman. Thus the illustrated *Haggadot* provide material for an interesting study of the professions that were considered unsuitable for Jewish boys in different places and at different times.

Detail of a page from the *Parma Haggadah* showing two of the four sons. On top is the wise son holding a scroll and below is the wicked son dressed in armor.

Opposite. Two illustrations from the *Joel ben Shimon Haggadah,* showing the simple son reading and the son who does not know to ask, looking at himself in a mirror.

The Story

After this prologue, comes the story of the Exodus. The Mishnah states that the narration should begin with the humiliating parts of Jewish history and only afterwards come to a glorious climax. However there was disagreement between two of the rabbis of the Talmud — whether the story should begin with the fact that "We were slaves to Pharaoh in Egypt...," emphasizing the physical slavery of the Jewish nation, or whether it should begin: "In the beginning our forefathers were idolators," which emphasized the abysmal spiritual state of the Israelites before they attained their national and religious freedom at the time of the Exodus. In fact both of these passages appear in the *Haggadah.* "We were slaves..." is said in answer to the four questions, and the story commences here with the idol-worshipping family of Abraham. Some scholars are of the opinion that beginning the story with the Patriarchs not only proves the antiquity of the Jewish nation, but is also a clever piece of political maneuvering, as discussed above.

The narrative tells of the patriarchal beginnings, and of God's promise to Abraham that his descendants would be strangers in a land which was not theirs, and that they would there become slaves. It relates how his grandson Jacob took his whole family down to Egypt for a short visit and how his descendants were to stay there and become slaves. The suffering of the Israelites in Egypt is dealt with a little more fully. Then details are given of

the liberation from Egypt by God Himself — "He and no other" — and of the terrible retribution He inflicted upon the Egyptians, and the plagues that He brought upon them. Detail and elaboration are provided by way of midrashic interpretations of the Scriptural verses cited. The liberation in itself would have been sufficient reason for praising God and being grateful to Him; He also sustained the Israelites in the wilderness, gave them the Torah and brought them to the Promised Land. A song is sung on this theme with a chorus consisting of the word *Dayyenu* ("It would have been sufficient for us!").

When the plagues of Egypt are mentioned, it is customary to spill some wine from the second cup. The reason for this being *Spilling Drops of Wine* that although the plagues killed the oppressors, sadness should still be felt at human suffering. The joy cannot be complete; the wine cup will not be full. 16 drops are spilt; three drops when the "blood, fire and pillars of smoke" that God sent down are mentioned, a drop for each of the ten plagues, and a drop for each of the three abbreviations that Rabbi Judah coined, consisting of the first letter of each of the ten plagues. These were given either as a mnemonic, or to show the pattern of the three sets of three plagues, each of increasing intensity, which are climaxed by the death of the firstborn in the tenth plague.

The song *"Dayyeinu"* written in zoomorphic letters and illustrated with grotesques, from the *Mocatta Haggadah,* Spain, 13th cent.

Woodcut illustrations for *Had Gadya*, from the haggadah by Jacob Steinhardt, 1923.

Interestingly, despite the **part that Moses played in the Exo-** *Moses not* dus, his name does not appear in the *Haggadah*, expect for one *Mentioned* passing instance. This is in order to stress that God Himself — "He and not a messenger" — had intervened in the history of the Jews. This reason also coincides with the desire of the rabbis to underplay the role of Moses, albeit the greatest of the prophets, to ensure that he would never be deified for performing miracles, as heroes of other religions were. In the Karaite *Haggadah* Moses is mentioned several times.

Afikoman

At the very end of the meal, the *afikoman* is recovered from its hiding place, or ransomed from the children who may have "stolen" it, and all participants eat a piece of it. This is the last food eaten on this night; it is followed by Grace after Meals, after which the third cup of wine is drunk.

Hymns of Praise

After the recitation of Grace after Meals the remainder of *Hallel* (Psalms 115-118) is chanted, followed by the "great *Hallel*" (Psalm 136), and *Nishmat,* a hymn which begins with the words "Let the soul of every living thing bless Thy name. . . . " For this night, commemorating the great liberation, is the time most fitting for praise. The fourth cup of wine is then drunk and "the order of the Passover is terminated according to all its statutes and laws." Thereupon all those who have participated in the *seder* express the wish: "Next year in Jerusalem! " If they are already in Jerusalem, they sing "Next year in Jerusalem the rebuilt! " To all intents and purposes this is the end of the *seder*.

Additional Hymns

In Ashkenazi communities further hymns are sung. These were included in the *Haggadah* as an incentive to encourage children to stay awake for the singing at the end. Most of the songs do not appear in the *Haggadot* of the Sephardi and Yemenite communities.

It Came to Pass at Midnight. The hymn with the refrain "And it came to pass at midnight" was probably composed in the 7th century c.e. by Yannai, the mentor of Eliezer Kallir. It tells how certain great events took place in the middle of the night: Jacob wrestled with the angel at night, the firstborn were killed at night, Belshazzar saw the writing on the wall at night, and so on. And the Messiah will come on a day which is neither day nor night, and will remove all darkness.

On Passover. In this hymn, Eliezer Kallir, a poet of the 8th century, tells of the important events that all happened "on Passover." Abraham welcomed the three angels who gave him the news of the impending birth of a son "on Passover." Sodom was destroyed and Lot saved "on Passover." The Egyptian firstborn were killed, Gideon was victorious, Haman was hanged, all "on Passover."

Mighty in Kingship. Then follow two litanies which list the divine attributes; neither contains any direct reference to Passover. The first lists the divine attributes in the first two lines of the strophe, and follows this with a list of the various angels who sing "To Thee and to Thee. . . . To Thee O God is the kingship, for Him it is proper to praise, for Him it is due." This poem was probably written in the 13th century in Germany, and its initial letters form an alphabetic acrostic.

Mighty is He. The second litany "Mighty is He" has appeared in Western European printed texts since the 16th century. It lists alphabetically the qualities of God ("Mighty is He, Blessed is He, Great is He, and so on") and follows these at intervals with a refrain imploring Him to rebuild the Temple speedily. In some Ashkenazi traditions the tune of this song is woven into other parts of the Passover liturgy, including Hallel, Kiddush and the priestly benediction.

Who knows One? One of the most popular songs, especially among children, begins with the words "Who knows One? " The answer given is: "I know One, One is our God in the heavens and on earth." The questions go up to thirteen, and the answers all have a religious content: "two are the tablets of the Law, three are the patriarchs," and so on. Some editions have been censored, and "eight are the days of circumcision" was changed to "eight are the lights of Ḥanukkah." Likewise, "nine are the months of pregnancy" became "nine are the festivals." This song is first found in a *Haggadah* of the 16th century, and is very similar to the German pastoral song *Guter freund, ich frage dich,* though counting songs are universal. Thus the English song "Who'll sing me one, ho, green grow the rushes, oh! " is answered by "One is One and all alone and ever more shall be so." This song in the *Haggadah* is in fact didactic and contains no specific reference to Passover. Indeed, Jews of Ceylon and Cochin sang it at weddings for the entertainment of newly-married couples.

An Only Kid. The last song, in Aramaic, tells of "an only kid (Ḥad Gadya) that father bought for two coins," but the kid is eaten by a cat, which is bitten by a dog, which is beaten by a stick, which is then burnt by fire, which is extinguished by water, which in turn is drunk by an ox, which is then slaughtered by a slaughterer, who is in turn killed by the Angel of Death — until God brings the final retribution. This song first appears in a *Haggadah* printed in the 16th century, and it seems to have been based upon the German folksong *Der Herr der schickt den Jockel aus,* though a similar motif appears in some Persian and Indian poems. This song was included in the *Haggadah* for the amusement of children, but some mystics have interpreted it as an allegory representing the various levels of the soul. Others have seen it as an allegory in which the one and only kid symbolizes the oppressed Jewish people which father (God) bought for two coins (Moses and Aaron). The oppressors of Israel are those that destroy, but who in turn are destroyed. The cat represents Assyria, the dog — Babylon, the stick — Persia, the fire — Macedonia, the water — Rome, the Ox — the Saracens, the slaughterer — the Crusaders, the Angel of Death — the Turks who ruled Palestine. The end of the song expresses hope for the Messianic redemption. God destroys the foreign rulers of the Holy Land and vindicates Israel, "the only kid." On the rousing final chorus of this song the *seder* comes to an end.

An' what of the country that we have left? In spite of the corruption an' rottenness that lie beneath the surface, we love this country of big buildings, with zooming elevators, of mountains an' deserts, universities an' museums, hot 'og stands an' soda fountains, white highways an' screeching trains, this immense land where everything comes in at least three sizes an' five brands, this sprawling nation that lies like some beautiful but 'umb body stretching from one ocean to another, with its head in the East, its warm bosom in the mid-west an' its muscular legs in the far-west. An' yet, without a doubt we are Jews an' will always be Jews.

An' now we 'in this potato in salt water, which symbolizes the crossing of the dead sea by our forefathers, an' the crossing of the great ocean in our 'wn time, whereby we reached our land.

The road to Sasa is a long one. It leads through the norts of 'urope, on ships loaded beyon' capacity through war an' peace an' the valley of the Shadow.

One year ago, on the very 'atc of our hityashvut, some of our chaverim broke through to the homeland from the Cyprus camps— an' with this they concluded a chapter of their lives an' of our kibbutz—illegal aliyah. We, the wholesome-healty youth, that 'id not pay the bitter 'rice for our Jewishness, we fulfilled our obligation in another way—illegal ali' '. Tiny shattered ships, broken, ugly, won'erful refugees. Small ships armed with courage— Wedgewood, Biria, Jewish State, Exodus—ships of Aliyah Bet.

A kibbutz *Haggadah* illustrating the passage "In every generation people have risen up against us. . ." The illustrator depicts an Egyptian, a Roman, a Crusader, a cossack and a Nazi (right). *Haggadah* from Kibbutz Sasa rewritten for early American settlers in Israel, 1949 (left).

The Kibbutz Haggadah

The *seder* that has been described above follows the traditional religious arrangement. In non-religious kibbutzim in Israel an elaborate public *seder* is held with music and dancing for members, children and guests at which their own kibbutz *Haggadah* is read. The *Haggadah* compiled by kibbutz Yagur is the prototype for all kibbutzim. It is based on the theme of the Exodus from Egypt, but it also includes events of a similar nature pertinent to modern Jewish history and kibbutz life, as well as appropriate passages from modern Hebrew literature. Many radical groups in America have also compiled their own *Haggadot* including additional passages from various sources, on topics that are considered appropriate; liberation and freedom are popular themes.

Texts

The *Haggadah* was apparently compiled by the *geonim* as a separate work in the seventh or eighth century. However, the oldest extant version is in the prayer book (*siddur*) of Saadiah Gaon (10th century); other early versions are found in *Maḥzor Vitry* (11th century) and in Maimonides' *Mishneh Torah* (12th century). Many recensions, differing from one another to a greater or lesser degree, have been preserved in various manuscripts, mostly dating from the 13th and 15th centuries, and also in fragments from the Cairo *Genizah*. These manuscripts originate from all countries in which Jews have lived. The earliest known edition of the *Haggadah* to be printed separately was produced in Spain in Guadalajara, c. 1482. It is reckoned that at least 3,000 editions have been printed since then, many of them illustrated, for the *Haggadah* has constantly been one of the most popular works — perhaps the most popular — in Jewish religious literature. Translations into Jewish vernaculars included Yiddish, Ladino, Judeo Greek, Judeo-Arabic (in its various dialects) and Judeo-Persian.

Many commentaries have been written on this comparatively small book. The earliest commentaries were written in a talmudic style and can be found in halakhic works of the school of Rashi (11th century) and his disciples. After the 15th century many commentators included discussions on the philosophical and theological contents, not always directly connected with the text; mystical commentaries were also written. Some editions of the *Haggadah* include as many as 200 commentaries, and new commentaries are still being written.

An Art Form
Jewish art was generally restricted by the prohibition contained in the Torah against making images: "Thou shalt not make unto thee a graven image, nor any manner of likeness, of any thing that is in heaven above, or that is in the earth beneath." This restriction was often relaxed in the case of the *Haggadah*, whose sanctity is less than that of Scripture. Yet the prohibition was not always completely ignored. Thus, in an illustrated *Haggadah* of the 13th century, known as the Birds' Head *Haggadah*, many figures have birds' heads, so as to avoid drawing the human image. There are also marked differences between the Sephardi *Haggadot* which were illustrated in a Muslim environment in which there were also prohibitions on the making of images, and those of Europe.

During the 13th to 15th centuries, the *Haggadah* was one of the most popular Hebrew illuminated manuscripts because of several factors. The social and economic growth of town life in Europe during the 13th century, brought prosperity to many Jews. It also fostered an increased interest in learning and art. The *Haggadah*, which was used for the most important domestic family ritual, had been separated from the *siddur* and so was a small book, which made it not too laborious to illustrate and not too expensive to commission. Even so, not every household could afford to possess an illuminated *Haggadah*. Only the richer Jews who, especially in Spain, were employed by princes or their

Detail from the *First Nuremberg Haggadah* showing textual illumination of an initial-word.

82

The Binding of Isaac (Gen. 22) in the *Birds' Head Haggadah*. Biblical illustrations were a common occurrence in illuminated *haggadot*.

courtiers and were therefore better acquainted with beautifully illuminated codices, could have the means to attempt the imitation of this fashion. The artist would generally tackle his commission by fusing traditional Jewish themes, motifs and iconography with the more fashionable styles and layout of contemporary Christian illumination, according to the taste of his patron.

The range of illumination that emanated from the Spanish, Ashkenazi (French and German) and Italian schools, can be roughly divided into four categories. There was textual illumination in which letters and words were decoratively illustrated. There were ritual illustrations in which whole series of pictures of ritual performances appear, for the most part didactic; the baking of *mazzot*, the family sitting around the *seder* table, the drinking of the four cups, and the like. These illustrations provide an interesting picture of the customs and clothes of various medieval European communities. The third kind of illumination was biblical illustrations. The last type, eschatological illustrations, portrayed the ultimate destiny of the Jewish people; in these Elijah is a very popular subject. In the second Nuremberg *Haggadah* he can be seen riding on a donkey with the Israelites following him to Jerusalem. The phrase beginning "Pour out Thy wrath upon

An illustration from the *Barcelona Haggadah*, Spain, 14th cent., showing the washing of hands.

the nations. . . " is often illustrated; in one text an angel can be seen at work, pouring the contents of the cup of retribution over a group of people.

Humor was not lacking from these illustrated *Haggadot*. In one text the passage "This bitter herb. . . " is accompanied by the picture of a man **point**ing to his wife.

A man points to his wife while reciting the passage on the bitter herbs. Detail from a miniature in a 14th cent. Spanish *Haggadah*.

The coming of the prophet Elijah, from the *Washington Haggadah*, Italy, 1478 (right).

Examples of Illuminated Haggadot

The Birds' Head Haggadah is so named because many of the human figures are depicted with birds' heads, though the artist used additional methods of human distortion, such as the depiction of a boy with a bulbous nose, angels with blank faces, and Egyptians in helmets with lowered visors. It was copied in South Germany late in the 13th century by a scribe named Isaac and is probably the oldest surviving Ashkenazi illuminated *Haggadah* manuscript. The style of illumination, the bright colors and the decorative motifs, though somewhat primitive, indicate its Upper Rhenish origin. It was discovered in 1946 by Mordekhai Narkiss, and reproduced in facsimile in 1967.

The Darmstadt Haggadah is an early 15th century manuscript preserved in the Darmstadt landesbibliothek. It was copied about 1430 by Israel ben Meir of Heidelberg in square Ashkenazi script. The illustrations consist mainly of teachers with male and female

84

בּוֹר הַמַּיִם עֲלֵיהֶם
אֲשֶׁר לֹא יְדַעֲרֹעֵל
הַמַּמְלָבוּת אֲשֶׁר בִּשֵׁמְךָ

86

students, some in small frames and others in many-storied gothic frames. A hunting scene is one of the pictures in the two full-page miniatures. A facsimile reproduction was produced in 1927 in Leipzig.

The Golden Haggadah is the earliest and most sumptuous of the illuminated Sephardi *Haggadot.* It contains the full text of the *Haggadah,* a collection of 100 liturgical poems, and 15 full-page miniatures illustrating the Bible, from Adam naming the animals, to the Exodus from Egypt. The style of the miniatures and the text illustrations suggest that it was executed in Barcelona in the first quarter of the 14th century. It was reproduced in facsimile in London in 1970.

Full page miniature from the *Darmstadt Haggadah,* Germany, 15th cent (left).

Full page miniature of the Creation from the *Sarajevo Haggadah,* Spain, 14th cent.

The Sarajevo Haggadah is a 14th-century Spanish illuminated manuscript which is the best-known of all Hebrew manuscripts. There are 34 pages of miniatures which display the widest range of subjects, from the Creation of the World, to Moses blessing Joshua and the Israelites before his death, followed by Illustrations of the Temple, preparations for Passover, and the interior of a Spanish synagogue. That the Sarajevo *Haggadah* originates from the kingdom of Aragon can be inferred from three coats of arms displayed in the manuscript. It reached the Sarajevo Museum in 1894 when a child of the city's Sephardi Jewish community brought it to school to be sold after his father had died, leaving the family destitute.

Printed Haggadot

The continuous record of the illustrated printed *Haggadah* begins with the Prague edition of 1526, which is among the finest productions of the 16th century press. The cuts and illustrations were long imitated, deteriorating progressively as the years went by.

The Mantua Edition (1560) reproduced the text of the Prague edition page for page and letter for letter in facsimile, but introduced new illustrations and marginal decorations which had already been used in non-Jewish publications and were in conformity with Italian taste. It was produced in facsimile in 1969 in Jerusalem. The first printed *Haggadah* to be consistently and systematically illustrated was produced in Venice, which had become the great center of Jewish publishing, at the turn of the 17th century (1599, 1601, 1603, and 1604). The Venice edition is largely based on the Mantua edition, and was widely imitated in southern Europe. The Amsterdam Edition (1695) closely followed the Venetian prototype, but the illustrations were improved by being engraved on copper. The Amsterdam editions had an enduring influence on *Haggadot* produced in the Ashkenazi world. Imitations have appeared since the 18th century with increasing indistinctness, until the present day.

The Seder Plate

While the *Haggadah* by its presence and use dominates the *seder* table, other manifestations of the artistic impulse are by no means lacking. The other most important item on the Passover table is the *seder*-plate. Illuminated medieval Ashkenazi *Haggadot* show a large round plate on the table, whereas in some Sephardi and Italian manuscripts a wicker basket is shown. Extant *seder*-plates from the time of the Renaissance and onward have been made of practically every material: wood, copper, pewter and porcelain, stoneware and plastics. Plates are frequently adorned with Passover scenes; Hebrew inscriptions are also popular. The earliest ceramic plates for Passover were probably made in Spain.

Seder in an 18th-century Bohemian home. Frontispiece to the *"Sister" to the Van Geldern Haggadah,* written and illuminated by the Moravian artist, Moses Leib ben Wolf of Trebitsch, 1716-17.

Above: Glazed ceramic *seder* dish, with scenes from the Exodus
alternating with Passover symbols. Erez Israel, 19th-century.
Opposite: Majolica *seder* dish, Spain, c. 1450. Some of the Hebrew
words are misspelled.

The poem *Dayyeinu* from the *Rylands Spanish Haggadah*. Th[e] architectural form within decorated panels. A hare hunt is a[n]

עשה כאהיהם
הרג כבוריהם
הרג כבוריהם
נתן לנו את ממונם
נתן לנו את ממונם
קרע לנו את הים
קרע לנו את הים
העבירנו כתוכ בחרב
העבי כתוכ בחרב
שקע צרינו בתוכו
שקע צרינו בתוכו
ספק צר נמ ארב שנ
ספק צר נמ אר שנ
האכילנו את המן

מה אומ אומ מה העדות והמשפטים ופי עוה
זן גבריד שהיא מדכם שטוא מ דיוע אנ מטבעלין קד ס
כליות ואנוזיי קדם מעדרה שמחלקין להם כל שישאל

קימים כלל להבא חל ל לית
שהינג נהי ישאלה
סעודי וסי זוע אנ אוזלי

vords of each verse are written one below the other in an
many grotesques depicted in the margins. Spain, 14th century.

Velvet *mazzah* cover embroidered with fish scales. There are three pockets in each of which a *mazzah* is placed. The cover is so made as to enable the celebrant to uncover the top *mazzah* at various points in the *seder* ceremony. Hungary, 19th century.

Clockwise from top left. A page from the *Prague Haggadah* (1526). Title page of the *Venice Haggadah* (1609). Title page of the *Amsterdam Haggadah* (1695). Title page of the *Mantua Haggadah* (1560).

89

A silver and glass tiered Passover plate, Denmark, 1918.

There are also blue Delft plates inscribed *"Pesaḥdic"* or *"Yontef-dic"*. An interesting type of *seder*-plate is the three-tiered open one with a silver frame and glass tiers so that the three *mazzot* are visible, whilst the decorative receptacles for the five items were placed on the top.

The Goblets

The wine goblets for *Kiddush* and for the ritual four cups are often artistically decorated, particularly Elijah's cup. The favorite theme here is the return to Zion. Other objects used at the *seder* also receive artistic attention: the cloth to cover the *mazzot*, the towel for drying the hands, the pillow for father to recline on, and the white robe for him to wear, were often embroidered with decorative designs.

Music

The chanting and singing of the *Haggadah* is observed in all Jewish communities, each one according to its own peculiar style and custom. The text offers opportunities for solo chant as well as for responsorial and community singing. Ashkenazi readers often use melodies close to the form of the synagogue chant, the *Adonai Malakh Shteiger,* while Jews from Iraq employ the *Tefil-*

A candle holder for the search for leaven; Ilya Schor, New York, c. 1950.

lah mode of prayer for some chapters. However, tunes vary from family to family, and constitute a still unexplored treasure of folklore. Some of the melodies used at the *seder* were also used as theme melodies for parts of the synagogue liturgy throughout Passover.

6. THE TIME OF SINGING IS COME

The basic synagogue liturgy for Passover is almost identical to that for the two other pilgrim festivals, Pentecost (Shavu'ot) and Tabernacles (Sukkot). The festival is referred to as the "Feast of Unleavened Bread" and described as the "time of our freedom." However, there are some differences, and some additions have been made that are considered appropriate for the season.

The Prayer for Dew
On the morning of the first day of Passover a special prayer for dew is said, which among Ashkenazim is called *Tefilat Tal*, and among Sephardim *Tikun Tàl*. In Israel, Passover always occurs in spring which comes at the end of the rainy season and at the beginning of the long dry summer, when the land is dependent on dew. As the fall of dew was considered to be a heavenly blessing just like rainfall and its absence a divine punishment, in Ashkenazi synagogues the reader wears a *kitel* (white robe) as on the Days of Awe, and he intones the *Kaddish* before *Musaf* in the same melody that is used on the Day of Atonement.

In the Ashkenazi rite the prayer consists of a series of acrostic poems. The central poem was written in the 8th century by Eliezer Kallir, and ends with the invocation:

"For Thou art the Lord our God who causes the wind to blow and the dew to descend,"

and with the plea:

"For a blessing and not for a curse;
For life and not for death;
For plenty and not for famine."

After this prayer has been said, it is the custom in Israel (and also amongst Sephardi communities in the Diaspora) to insert the phrase *morid ha-tal* ("who causes the dew to descend") at the beginning of the second benediction in every *Amidah* (standing prayer), until the prayer for rain is recited in the autumn.

The Omer

Passover is the "festival of spring," and in Temple times special ceremonies took place to mark the new harvest. The Torah ordains that a sheaf of the first grain was to be brought to the Temple. (The word for sheaf is *omer* in Hebrew, but was here interpreted by the rabbis to mean a measure of grain.) "On the morrow after the day of rest the priest shall wave it," holding the sheaf in outstreatched arms whilst moving from side to side. A handful was burnt at the altar, and the rest eaten by the priest. Until this ceremony had taken place it was forbidden to eat of the new harvest. The *Omer* ceremony was performed to protect the harvest from injurious winds and other calamities.

The Torah also ordained that the 49 days from Passover to Shavu'ot should be counted: "And ye shall count unto you from the morrow after the day of rest, from the day that ye brought the sheaf of waving; seven weeks shall there be complete; even unto the morrow after the seventh week shall ye number fifty days." The "morrow after the day of rest" (*Shabbat* in Hebrew) was taken to mean the day after the first holy day of Passover. There was a heated controversy over this, the Sadducees and later the Karaites taking "the day of rest" to mean the Sabbath. They would therefore start counting on Sunday, so that for Karaites, Shavu'ot always occurs on that day.

The Counting of the *Omer, Sefirat ha-Omer*, begins on the second night of Passover, and for 49 nights the number of days

A parchment scroll indicating the counting of the *omer,* made before 1730.

Symbolic reaping of the *omer* at kibbutz Ramat Yohanan, 1960 (below).

and weeks is counted until seven weeks are completed; the fiftieth day is Shavu'ot, the Feast of Weeks, and the "time of the giving of the Torah." Kabbalists held that the counting of the 49 days of the *Omer* symbolically represented the ascent out of the 49 gates of impurity. The Exodus from Egypt marked the beginning of the ascent, which was completed before the giving of the Torah at Mount Sinai seven weeks later. Similarly, the individual's ascent out of the 49 gates of impurity must be completed every year before he receives the Torah again on Shavu'ot.

The agricultural character of the traditional Jewish festivals is emphasized in kibbutz celebrations. In the 1920s and 1930s the kibbutz movement attempted to revive ancient Hebrew traditions

The Omer in the Kibbutz

that were connected with the land and with agriculture and over the years these Jewish holidays acquired a tradition of their own as the settlers became aware of the need for festive occasions, both as an educational experience for their children and to relieve the monotony of daily life. An *Omer* festival based on biblical and mishnaic sources was inaugurated, coinciding with the harvesting of the first ripe grain. Thus on the day before Passover, kibbutz members and their children go singing and dancing into the fields. A number of ears of grain are ceremonially cut, to be placed in the dining hall as part of the Passover celebrations.

The Song of Songs
The biblical book of the Song of Songs is considered appropriate for reading on Passover because of its associations with spring. This book consists essentially of a series of lyrical songs in which two lovers sing to one another of the delights and anguish of their love. The rabbis understood the book as an allegory for the love between God and His people. Passover is the springtime of this love:

> "For, lo, the winter is past,
> The rain is over and gone;
> The flowers appear on the earth;
> The time of singing is come,
> And the voice of the turtle is heard in our land;
> The fig-tree putteth forth her green figs,
> And the vines in blossom give forth their fragrance,
> Arise, my love, my fair one, and come away."

There was much controversy in the second century over whether this book should be included in the canon of the Bible. Rabbi Akiva held: "All the books of the Bible are holy, but this is the holy of holies."

In Ashkenazi communities it is read on the intermediate Sab- **94** bath of Passover, and if there is no intermediate Sabbath, on the first day of the festival. It is read during the morning service prior to the reading of the *Torah*. In the Sephardi ritual it is read before the Afternoon Service on the last day. In some communities it is also read at the *seder* after the *Haggadah* has been completed.

Hallel

On the other pilgrim festivals, *Hallel*, songs of praise to God consisting of Psalms 113-118, is chanted throughout the festival. However, for the last six days of Passover, two portions are omitted, the first half of Psalm 115 and the first half of Psalm 116, so that only half of *Hallel* is chanted. This is because the joy of the festival is marred by the disaster that befell the Egyptian host that was drowned at the victorious crossing of the Red Sea.

Page from the *Sarajevo Haggadah,* showing (at top) the Israelites crossing the Red Sea and Pharaoh's men drowning, and (at bottom) Miriam and the women of Israel dancing during the chanting of the Song of the Sea, Spain, 14th cent.

95

The Song of the Sea

The crossing of the Red Sea, or the "Sea of Reeds," and the drowning of the Egyptian host, took place seven days after the Israelites left Egypt. Consequently, on the seventh day of Passover it is customary to read from the Torah the portion that contains the triumphant Song of the Sea that was sung by "Moses and the Children of Israel... when the waters returned and covered the chariots and horsemen, even all the host of Pharaoh." The song is chanted to a special melody. Because the miracle occurred at night, it is customary for some hasidic sects to chant this song at a special ceremony at midnight, preferably near the sea; in Tel Aviv large crowds assemble at the beach on this last night of Passover to sing the Song of the Sea.

7. THE LORD BROUGHT US OUT OF EGYPT

The ceremonies that have been described are those of the mainstream of Jewry. The Samaritans, the Karaites, and the Falashas, also observe Passover, though with interesting differences.

Samaritans

The Samaritans offer the Paschal sacrifice even nowadays according to the laws stated in the Pentateuch. In 1972 eighteen lambs were slaughtered on Mount Gerizim near Nablus, for the community of 445 persons. According to the Bible the Samaritans originated from a mixture of the people who were living in Samaria and others who were transported there, in an exchange of populations at the time of the conquest of Samaria by Assyria in 722/1 b.c.e. However, their own chronicles claim that they are direct descendants of the Joseph tribes Ephraim and Manasseh, and that they have occupied their ancient territory in central Israel continuously. They also claim that the schism with other Jews was effected by Eli the high priest about the year 1080 b.c.e. when he moved the cult to Shiloh from Shechem (Nablus)

The Samaritan high priest, Avisha ben Phinehas (center) and notables of the community during the prayer of the Passover sacrifice.

where the Samaritan center still exists nowadays. The principal source for their laws is the Pentateuch. Thus on the tenth day of the first month of Nisan, which due to their different calendar occurs about a month later than the more widely accepted Nisan, the entire community assembles on the slopes of the "chosen mountain," Mount Gerizim, where they live until the end of the festival. At twilight on the 14th all the members gather at the site of the altar which is about 800 yards from the summit. They arrive in two groups; the first group performs the sacrifice, and the second group recites prayers. At a signal from the high priest who stands on a large stone, the sheep are slaughtered amidst the cries of the congregation raised in prayer. After the *kashrut* has been checked and the wool plucked, the sheep are rinsed and salted and then laid aside for two hours until the blood has been absorbed by the salt.

At about 8 o'clock in the evening the sheep are carried on spits and placed into ovens that have been dug in the earth. At midnight the celebrants return with bowls, remove the sheep, and divide the meat into bowls. Each family takes its portion to its house on the mountain where it quickly eats the sacrifice together with *mazzot* and bitter herbs. Anything that is left over is returned to the altar and burned.

Karaites

The Karaites do not offer up the Paschal sacrifice nowadays since they are of the opinion that this sacrifice can only be performed in the Temple in Jerusalem. This opinion is based on the Bible which they regard as the only source of all their laws, for they refuse to accept the Talmud as authoritative. This refusal is the reason for the schism with Rabbanite Jews in the 8th and 9th centuries. The main centers of Karaism are now in Crimean Russia where there are about 18,000, and there are about 8,000 in Israel.

The Karaites observe Passover for seven days, starting on the fifteenth of the first month of Nisan, which according to their calendar varies only slightly from the normative date for Passover. Before Passover they dispose of all their *hamez*, though they do not prohibit *hamez* which should be found to have been in their possession during Passover, as do the Rabbanites. They also eat *mazzah* for seven days, and on the *seder* night they read their own *Haggadah* which is composed mainly of quotations from the Bible and *piyyutim*. Unlike the Rabbanites' text, there are quite a few references to Moses in their *Haggadah*. They also eat *maror* despite the fact that according to the Pentateuch this is to be eaten with the Paschal sacrifice. However, the eating of *maror* is decreed by tradition, the *Sevel ha-Yerushah* ("Yoke of Inheritance"), which supplements the laws they derive from the Bible.

Falashas

There are now about 30,000 Falashas living in N. Ethiopia. According to their tradition they descend from the notables of Jerusalem who accompanied Manasseh the son of King Solomon from his union with the Queen of Sheba, when he returned to

98

Ethiopia. However, most scholars believe that they are a segment of the indigenous Agau population which was converted to Judaism through the influence of Jews from Egypt or from S.W. Arabia. The word Falasha comes from a word meaning "emigrate" in the Ge'ez language which is the language of their literature, although they speak Amharic; they refer to themselves as *Beta Israel,* the house of Israel. They believe in the One God of Israel who has chosen His people, and who will send the Messiah to return them to the Holy land; the immigration authorities of Israel are not as yet encouraging this move. The Jewish practices that they observe are based on the Bible, and have been recorded by travellers who were present at their celebrations.

They celebrate Passover, or *Fasika (feseh),* from the fifteenth to the twenty-first day of the first moon. On the eve of Passover a sacrificial lamb is slaughtered. Throughout the seven days of the festival nothing may be eaten or drunk which has become leavened or fermented or which has been kept overnight. They eat a special unleavened bread *(qita)* and drink only coffee or a special beverage called *celqa* which is made of water mixed with flour or other seeds. Milk is drunk as soon as it is taken from the cow, because once it is creamy it is considered fermented and must be given to the animals or thrown away. During the festival special prayers are said, accompanied by beatings of the drum and the sounding of the gong. The first and last days are called holy days, and no work or travel of any kind is allowed. The intermediate days do not have any special name, but the people do not work then. However, they may go from one village to another to visit relatives and friends.

At the end of Passover, the first beer brewed and the first bread baked are brought to the synagogue and given to the priest as offerings. The priest blesses the bread and eats it while the congregation recite the Ten Commandments from memory.

Maimuna

The end of the Passover and the baking of the first bread are also celebrated by the Jews of North Africa, in particular those of Morocco. On the evening that Passover ends and for the following day they celebrate the *Maimuna*. The origin of this word is obscure. According to tradition Maimon the father of Maimonides, who once lived in Fez, died on the last day of Passover. Since death is seen as being a reunion of man with his Creator, a celebration is held on the anniversary of the death; in this case it was postponed until the day after the festival so that the two celebrations should not coincide. Some connect the word with the Hebrew *emunah* meaning belief. Thus the celebration is a demonstration of belief in the redemption of Israel, and is held near Passover because "As the Children of Israel were redeemed in Nisan so will they be redeemed in the future in Nisan."

Others see the celebration as marking the new harvest and the beginning of the new financial year, and they connect the word *Maimuna* with a similar Arabic word meaning happiness or prosperity. People greet each other on this day with the words "May you be prosperous, and may you be happy! *(tirbah wa-tis'ad)*".

A Moroccan immigrant dancing at the Maimuna celebration in Jerusalem.

100

Pewter plate for Passover. On the rim is the order of the *seder,* and in the center an 8 pointed star, the four sons, and other figures. Germany, 1771 (left).

Ivory Passover goblet, Germany, 17/18 cent (right).

The central event of the celebrations used to be the baking of the first leavened bread after Passover. The yeast is considered symbolic of Israel, so efforts are made to ensure that it rises properly. In some communities the wine from the cup of Elijah is kept and poured over the yeast. When the dough is being prepared songs are sung that the rising bread should be a good omen.

It is the custom for people to visit each other on this night, and North African Jews in Israel delight in telling how their Muslim neighbors used to visit them on the *Maimuna.* Tables were laid with all kinds of food and drink; in the middle of the table there would be a bowl of water in which there was a fish, a symbol of fruitfulness and abundance. In every house people would partake of food and drink, sing and dance, and bless each other. In Morocco it was a custom to bless unmarried men and women that they should be married within the coming year.

On the following day outings would take place into the countryside, especially to places where there was water. It was the custom for people to pour water over their hands and feet and also on the threshold of their houses; this may be connected with the crossing of the Red Sea.

101

In Israel, where the majority of North African Jews emigrated, the *Maimuna* was celebrated only modestly at first. After it was seen that communal differences were not eradicated in the "melting pot," the celebrations were revived on a national scale, mainly by Moroccan Jews, as a token show of group solidarity.

8. THE TIME OF OUR FREEDOM

No event in Jewish history has had as great an influence on Judaism and Jewish thought through the ages as the Exodus from Egypt. A large number of the commandments in the Torah contain direct references to it; the rabbis were even to require that Jews should mention the Exodus in their prayers every day of their lives. God's direct intervention in the history of Israel, and the freedom that resulted from this, were considered to be the two most significant aspects.

God in History
It is an important doctrine that the Exodus from Egypt resulted from the direct intervention of God Himself, "He and no other." A definite concept of God in history is apparent in the Bible, and was later amplified in rabbinic theology. The God of Israel is the God of Abraham, Isaac and Jacob who is involved in human affairs; He is not merely an object of philosophical speculation. The Exodus is a clear manifestation of God as an historical force in the world. Thus the first of the Ten Commandments begins: "I am the Lord thy God who brought thee out of the Land of Egypt," rather than "I am the Lord thy God who created the heavens and the earth," emphasizing the intervention of God in Jewish history.

God and Israel
A corollary of this is the doctrine of the election of Israel. The Bible vividly portrays how Israel was chosen by God from all the

Page from the 14th cent. *Sassoon Spanish Haggadah,* with the passage "And the Lord brought us out of Egypt with a mighty hand and an outstretched arm." The Children of Israel, in medieval dress are depicted leaving a walled city.

nations, and acquired by Him, so to speak, by the act of the redemption from Egypt. This privilege involves reciprocal obligations; the verse "I will take you to Me for a people," continues "and I will be to you a God." He demanded obedience from His people, and they were to construct their society in accordance with His commandments. They were also to be God's torchbearers, "a light to the nations," even at the cost of their own suffering. In view of the fact that Christianity developed from Judaism, and Islam was influenced by both, it can be said that the majority of people who believe in One God do so as a result of the Exodus. Recalling the Exodus serves as a reminder of this, and also serves to arouse aspirations for the future when the whole world will be united in acceptance of the divine order: "And the earth shall be full of the knowledge of the Lord, as the waters cover the sea."

Inner Freedom

Passover also symbolizes freedom, for the Exodus was the culmination of the liberation from Egyptian slavery. The word freedom has been given many meanings. To be free can mean to be neither constrained nor under obligation — to be uninhibited. For rationalists, to be free is to live in conformity with the rational nature of man and of the universe. Erich Fromm has said that love is a state of transcending one's separateness, and liberating oneself from self-centeredness. True freedom, according to the rabbis is only to be found in the service of God: "Only he is free who occupies himself with Torah." They considered that man is constituted of two conflicting forces, an inclination to evil and an inclination to good. He is a free agent to choose to follow either, yet in the constant struggle between the conflicting forces, inner freedom is achieved by his overcoming the baser instincts and following the divine path. Yet freedom from subjection to others is necessary in order to be free to serve God; the Torah was given at Sinai only after the Exodus had taken place; some were to stress that the 49 days between these two events

104

was necessary to allow the mind and soul to become liberated from the effects of the slavery of the body.

Personal Freedom
An immediate consequence of such a doctrine of freedom must necessarily be respect for the personal freedom of others. No Jew is to be owned, even by another Jew. According to the Bible, he may be sold as a slave, in times when slavery was an accepted social phenomenon, only as a consequence of theft for which he is unable to make restitution, or in cases of extreme poverty, and only for six years; he was then to be so well treated that the Talmud remarks that "he who buys a slave, buys a master for himself." In the seventh year he was to be set free, but not empty-handed. "Thou shalt furnish him liberally out of thy flock and out of thy threshing floor, and out of thy wine-press. . . and thou shalt remember that thou wast a bondsman in the land of Egypt." However, should this Jewish slave not wish to go free, the Torah ordains that he should be punished, "His master shall bore his ear through with an awl; and he shall serve him for ever." The Talmud remarks: "Why the ear of all organs of the body? God said: Because it was the ear which heard Me say upon Mount Sinai, Unto Me are the children of Israel servants, but not servants to servants". The only reason a Jew may be employed by another Jew is that he preserves his liberty, since he maintains the right to withdraw his labor.

Even non-Jews who became Hebrew slaves were to be set free *Proclaim* in the Jubilee year: "And ye shall hallow the fiftieth year, and *Liberty* proclaim liberty throughout the land." The Hebrew word for liberty, *dror,* is the same word that is used for the swallow, a bird that recognizes no mastery; God is to be the only master of man.

The national experience of slavery in Egypt is also to make *Love the* Jews feel empathy for people in similar situations: "And you *Stranger* should know the soul of the stranger, for you were strangers in the land of Egypt." The Torah ordains that a stranger is not to be wronged or oppressed; on the contrary he is to be well received, even loved, "thou shalt love him as thyself, for ye were strangers in the land of Egypt."

National Freedom

Yet above all Passover is a festival of national freedom. The Exodus marks the beginnings of an independent Jewish nation, which was consolidated when they arrived in their homeland, the Land of Israel, where they lived for centuries under the kings David and Solomon and their descendants. When the First Temple was destroyed in 586 b.c.e., national independence was lost for a while, but after seventy years of exile, Jews again returned to Erez Israel to lay the foundations for an independent Jewish commonwealth. The Roman occupation of Judea which started in 37 b.c.e., did not put an end to national feeling. It has been suggested that the difference between the Zealots and the Pharisees with regard to the love of freedom was that whereas the Pharisees extolled the importance of liberty they did not include it among the cardinal principles for which one should suffer martyrdom rather than transgress; whereas the Zealots did include it. And according to Josephus, "they think little of submitting to death, if only they may avoid calling any man master," a principle which they carried into practice with their mass suicide at Masada rather than submit to the Romans.

The destruction of the second Temple by the Romans in 70 *Exile* c.e. and the subsequent dispersion of Jews through many parts of the world did not obliterate the intense yearning for renewed national independence. In fact some were to see the exile as proof of the impending national renewal.

Thus the Talmud relates that when Rabbi Akiva's disciples burst into tears at the sight of foxes prowling through the site of the despoiled Temple, he laughed. He explained that he was laughing because when he saw the fulfillment of the prophecy that Zion shall be ploughed as a field, he was reassured of the future fulfillment of the prophecy that Jerusalem will again be rebuilt. Others were to see the subjection of the Jewish people and the resultant suffering and degradation as part of a divine plan, an historical cycle in which subjection precedes liberation, similar to the enslavement in Egypt that preceded the Exodus — a necessary prelude to the ultimate freedom.

Yet throughout all the periods in which Jews were expelled from countries in which they were not accepted as citizens, and during all the periods that they were humiliated and persecuted, they continued to yearn. "This year we are here, next year in Erez Israel; this year we are slaves, next year free men" The annual festival of Passover contributed much to the ideal of free-

Glass Cup of Elijah. Bohemiah, 19th cent.

dom being kept alive in Jewish consciousness. The story of the Exodus is a perpetual source of hope for the future, and the ritual with which the story is told abounds in symbolism on this theme. *Mazzah* that is eaten because it is free from leaven, also symbolizes freedom, the four cups represent the four phases of subjection and the four stages of liberation of Israel, past and present, and then a cup of Elijah is filled to welcome the Messiah who will redeem Israel and remove the yoke of foreign rule. In fact according to one opinion in the Talmud, which is accepted by Maimonides, the only difference between the present world and the Messianic age is liberation from foreign rule.

Yet for all these aspirations, and despite the fact that it was an article of faith and an emotional necessity for Jews to believe in the advent of the Messiah, they were often lukewarm to messianic movements, even actively opposing them. Traditionally, deliverance was to be expected at times of exceptionally great suffering and international upheaval which were referred to as the "birth pangs" of the Messiah (*hevlei mashiah*). Even in these times the various messianic leaders could usually only gather a local following. The outstanding exception was Shabbetai Zevi (1626-1672) who was proclaimed as the Messiah in 1655 and acclaimed by Jews from all parts of Erez Israel and the Diaspora. The tremendous disappointment that overcame Jewry when he converted to Islam, made many Jews re-direct their utopian yearnings, and it was the opinion of Martin Buber that it was this messianic urge which was to make many Jews join the modern revolutionary movements. Others were later to participate in the secular Zionist movement and take practical steps towards the renewal of Jewish Independence.

Jewish national independence was eventually regained when the State of Israel was established in 1948, and Jews from all over the Dispersion began to flock to their homeland. This achievement was hailed by many traditional Jews as the *athalta de-geulah* (the beginnings of the messianic age). Thus the first part of the prophecy of Ezekiel is being fulfilled: "For I will take you from among the nations, and gather you out of all the countries, and will bring you into your own land."

Meaningful national freedom, however, requires the fulfillment of further conditions: "And I will put My spirit within you, and cause you to walk in My statutes," in a society built on social justice, on truth, and on peace. Thus, while Jews around the world sing toward the end of the *seder*, "Next year in Jerusalem," Jews in Israel, conscious of room for further improvement, make a slight addition: "Next year in Jerusalem the Rebuilt! "

The Western Wall on the anniversary of the reunification of Jerusalem, 28th day of the month of Iyyar.

Afikoman, a piece of *mazzah* put aside at the beginning of the *seder,* and eaten at the end of the meal.

Ashkenazi (pl. Ashkenazim), German or West-, Central-, or East-European Jew(s), as contrasted with Sephardi(m).

Geonim (sing. *gaon*), formal title of heads of academies in the post-Talmudic period.

Haggadah, (pl. *Haggadot*), narration, text read at the *seder.*

Hallel, songs of praise, Psalms 113-118.

Hamez, leavened bread and food, as well as dishes and cooking utensils used throughout the year, and forbidden for use on Passover.

Hanukkah, or The Festival of Lights, eight-day festival (commencing 25 Kislev-December) inaugurated by the rabbis after the victory of the Maccabees in 165 b.c.e.; an increasing number of lights is kindled each night.

Haroset, past made of wine, nuts and other ingredients, used at the *seder.*

Iyyar, second month of the Jewish calendar (April-May).

Kaddish, liturgical prayer in Aramaic.

Karpas, a vegetable dipped in salt water at the *seder.*

Kashering, method of cleansing *hamez* from vessels and utensils.

Kiddush, lit. "sanctification," prayer recited over a cup of wine to consecrate the Sabbaths and festivals.

Kitel, white robe, associated with purity, worn on solemn occasions.

Maror, a bitter herb.

Mazzah (pl. Mazzot), unleavened bread.

Mishnah, earliest codification of Jewish Oral Law, completed in the third century c.e.

Mitzvah, biblical or rabbinic injunction.

Musaf, additional prayer service on Sabbaths and festivals.

Nisan, first month of the Jewish calendar (March-April).

Omer, forty-nine days counted from the time that the first of the barley harvest was offered in the Temple (second day of Passover) until Shavuot.

Piyyut, liturgical poem.

Purim, joyous holiday celebrated on the fourteenth or fifteenth day of Adar (February-March), inaugurated by the rabbis on the basis of the Scroll of Esther.

Seder, the ceremony on the first night (in the Diaspora first two nights) of Passover.

Sephardi (pl. Sephardim), Jew(s) of Spain and Portugal and their descendants, wherever resident; often loosely used for Oriental Jews when contrasted with Ashkenazi(m).

110

Shavuot, Pentecost, or Feast of Weeks, pilgrim festival and agricultural festival on the anniversary of the giving of the Torah at Mount Sinai, celebrated for one day in Israel, two in the Diaspora, in Sivan (May-June).

Shofar, horn blown ceremonially on festive occasions; a ram's horn is generally used.

Siddur, prayer-book.

Sukkot, or Tabernacles, pilgrim festival and agricultural festival beginning on the fifteenth of Tishrei (September-October), celebrated for seven days in Israel, eight in the Diaspora.

Talmud, compendium of discussion on the Mishnah by generations of scholars and jurists in many academies over a period of several centuries.

ABBREVIATIONS TO SOURCES

BIBLE

Gen.	– Genesis	Jos.	– Joshua	Zech.	– Zechariah
Ex.	– Exodus	Jud.	– Judges	Ps.	– Psalms
Lev.	– Leviticus	Is.	– Isaiah	Cant.	– Canticles
Num.	– Numbers	Ezek.	– Ezekiel	Eccl.	– Ecclesiastes
Deut.	– Deuteronomy	Mic.	– Micah	Chron.	– Chronicles

TALMUD[1]

TJ	– Jerusalem Talmud[2]			Pes.	– *Pesahim*
BB	– *Baba Batra*	Kid.	– *Menahot*	Sanh.	– *Sanhedrin*
Ber.	– *Berakhot*	Men.	– *Menahot*	Ta'an.	– *Ta'anit*
Hag.	– *Hagigah*	Ned.	– *Nedarim*	Yev.	– *Yevamot*

LATER AUTHORITIES

Yad	– Maimonides, *Yad ha-Hazakah*
Sh.Ar.	– Shulhan Arukh
EH	– Even ha-Ezer
OH	– Orah Hayyim
YD	– Yoreh De'ah
Taz	– *Turei Zahav* to Shulhan Arukh
Davidson, Ozar	– I. Davidson, *Ozar ha-Shirah ve-ha-Piyyut*
Eisenstein, Dinim	– J.D. Eisenstein, *Ozar Dinim u-Minhagim* (1927; several reprints)

---

[1] References to the Mishnah are in the form Pes. 10:6 (i.e., Tractate *Pesahim*, chapter 10, mishnah 6); references to the Gemara are in the form: Pes. 64a (i.e. Tractate *Pesahim*, page 64, first side).

[2] Otherwise all Talmud references are to the Babylonian Talmud.

SOURCES

page

1   "passed over. . . " – Ex. 12:27

1   *Ḥag ha-Pesaḥ* – Ex. 34:25

1   *"Ḥag ha-Maẓẓot"* – Ex. 12:17

1   month of Aviv – Ex. 23:15

2   Dating the Exodus – M. Kasher, *Haggadah Shlemah,* Jerusalem, 1967, p. 120; Y Kaufman, *Toledot ha-Emunah ha-Yisre'elit,* vol. 2, p. 302-338 (for Habiru p.7, Hyksos, p. 5); W.F. Albright, *Bulletin of the American School of Oriental Research,* vol. 58, 1935

2   "And. . . Solomon. . . " – I Kings 1:6

2   300 years – Jud. 11:26

3   "And. . . even the selfsame. . . " – Ex. 12:41

3   "Pithom and Ramses" – Ex. 1:11

4   Josephus – Josephus, *Contra Apionem* 1:82-92

5   "stars of heaven. . . " – Gen. 22:18

5   "thy seed. . . " – Gen. 15:18

8   "the land was filled with them" – Ex. 1:7

8   "but the more they. . . " – Ex. 1:12

8   "Every son. . . " – Ex. 1:22

8   The Rabbinic commentators – cf. Naḥmanides to Ex. 1:23

8   "We cried. . . " – Deut. 26:7

8   "it was from the water . . . " – Ex. 2:10

9   "Let My people go!" – Ex. 5:1

12   "hardened his heart" – cf. Ex. 10:1

12   600,000 – Ex. 12:37; cf. Nahmanides

13   "God led them not – Ex. 13:17

14   Ibn Ezra – to Ex. 14:13

14   "the waters were a wall. . . " – Ex. 14:22

14   "the waters returned. . . " – Ex. 14:28

14   The Midrash – cf. Sanh. 39 b; Exodus Rabbah 15:7

16   "I will sing to. . . " – Ex. 15:1-2

16   "I am the Lord. . . " – Ex. 20:2

17   "Draw out. . . " – Ex. 12:21

17   "They shall eat. . . " – Ex. 12:8-11

17   "And it shall come to pass. . . " – Ex. 12:25-27

18   "that thou mayest. . . " – Deut. 16:3

18   "they kept. . . " – Num. 9:5

114

115

page

84   *The Darmstadt Haggadah* – cf. Italiener, B., *Die Darmstaedter Pessach-Haggadah*
          (1927-28)

87   *The Golden Haggadah* – cf. B. Narkiss, *The Golden Haggadah,* (1970)

87   *The Sarajevo Haggadah* – cf. C. Roth (ed.), *The Sarajevo Haggadah,* (1963)

88   Printed *Haggadot* – cf. A. Yaari, *Bibliografyah shel Haggodot Pesah,* 1960

91   "For Thou art the Lord. . . " – Davidson, Ozar, I, 236

92   "on the morrow. . . . " – Lev. 23:11

92   protect. . . from injurious winds – cf. Men. 62a

92   "And you shall count. . . " – Lev. 23:15

92   controversy. . . . Sadducees. . . – cf. Men. 65a

92   Counting of the *Omer* – Sh. Ar., OH 489

94   "For lo, the winter . . . " – Cant. 2:11

94   Rabbi Akiva held "All. . . . holy. . . . " – *Yada'im,* 3:5

95   half of Hallel – Sh. Ar., OH 490:4

96   "the waters returned. . . . " – Ex. 14:28

96   Samaritans, According to the Bible – II Kings, 17:24-41; cf. Macdonald, J.,
          The Theology of the Samaritans (1964); M. Gaster, *The Samaritans,* (1925)

97   community assembles. . . performs the sacrifice – cf. Montgomery, J.A.,
          The Samaritans, (1907), pp. 37ff.

98   Karaites observe Passover – cf. L. Nemoy, *The Karaite Anthology,* (1952),
          pp. 197-210

98   Falashas, scholars believe – cf. E. Ullendorf, in *Bulletin of the School of*
          Oriental and African Studies, University of London, 24 (1961), pp. 419-43

99   celebrate Passover – cf. W. Leslau, (ed.), *Falasha Anthology*)1951), p. xxxi

99   *Maimuna* – cf. H.Z. Hirschberg, *Me-Erez Mevo ha-Shemesh,* (1957), p. 77

102   rabbis . . . required – Ber. 1:5 based on Deut. 16:3

102   "He and no other" – Mechilta, *Bo,* 7, Ex. 20:2

102   "I am the Lord thy God . . . " – Ex. 20:2

104   "I will take . . . " and "I will be . . . " – Ex. 6:7

104   "a light to the nations" – Is. 42:6

104   "And the earth . . . " – Is. 11:9

104   "Only he is free . . . " – Avot 6:2

104   Erich Fromm – *The Art of Loving,* 1956, "The Theory of Love"

105   "He who buys a slave . . . " – Kid. 22a

105   "thou shalt furnish him . . . . " – Deut. 15:14

105   "His master shall bore . . . " Ex. 21:6

105   Talmud . . . "why the ear . . . " – Kid. 22b

105   "And ye shall hallow . . . " – Lev. 25:10

READING LIST

Encyclopaedia Judaica, Jerusalem, 1972, under: *Afikoman,* Exodus, *Haggadah, Ḥameẓ, Maẓẓah,* Messiah, Passover

Buber, Martin, *Moses,* Oxford and London, 1947.

Gaster, Theodor H., *Passover: Its History and Traditions,* New York, 1949.

Goldman, S., *Book of Human Destiny: From Slavery to Freedom,* New York, 1958.

Goodman, Philip, *The Passover Anthology,* Philadelphia, 1961.

Gordon, Albert I., *How to Celebrate Passover at Home,* New York, 1947.

Kaplan, Mordecai M. (ed.) and others, *The New Haggadah for the Pesah Seder,* New York, 1942.

Kasher, Menahem M. (ed.), *The Passover Haggadah,* New York, 1950.

Levy, Isaac, *A Guide to Passover,* London, 1952.

Lewittes, Mendel, *Passover,* New York.

Roth, C., *Ritual Murder Libel and the Jew,* London, 1934.

Schauss, H., *Guide to Jewish Holy Days,* New York, 1966.

Segal, J.B., *The Hebrew Passover,* London, 1963.

ILLUSTRATION CREDITS

Budapest, Library of Hungarian Academy of Sciences, facing p. 1
W. Flinders Petrie, *Six Temples at Thebes,* London, 1890, p. 3
London, British Museum, p. 6, 7, 10, 19, 34, 36, 52, 59, 66, 71, 75, 83, 84
Parma, Bibliotica Palatina, p. 9, 74
Jerusalem, Schocken Library, p. 13, 64, 82
Tel Aviv, Israel Government Press Office, p. 23, 29, 47, 62, 93
Jerusalem, Israel Department of Antiquities and Museums, p. 24
Photo D. Harris, Jerusalem, p. 28, 35, 39, 48, 55, 61, 63, 69, 70, 83, 100, 101, 109;
        color: pl. 2, 6, 8 (top), cover
Cincinatti, Hebrew Union College, p. 37; color: pl. 1
Amsterdam, Stedelijk Museum, p. 38
Jerusalem, Keren Hayesod, United Israel Appeal Photo Archives, p. 41
P.C. Kirchner, *Juedisches Ceremoniel . . . ,* Nuremberg, 1734, p.42
Jerusalem, Jewish National and University Library, p. 44, 89
J. Leusden, *Philologus Hebraeo-Mixtus,* Utrecht, 1663, p. 44
Basle, Jewish Museum, p. 45
Photo D. Widmer, Basle, p. 45
H. Grinstein, *The Rise of the Jewish Community in New York,* Philadelphia, 1945, p. 46
Photo W. Braun, Jerusalem, p. 47, 109
Jerusalem, Israel Museum, p. 48, 55, 56, 65, 70, 83, 90, 107;
        color: pl. 3, cover
New York, Oscar Gruss Collection, p.49
Photo F. Darmstaedter, New York, p. 49, 65, 90
Erlangen-Nuremberg, Universitaetsbibliothek, p. 51, 73
Formerly Detroit, Charles Feinberg Collection, p. 55
Photo Manning Bros., Highland Park, Michigan, p. 55
Photo Shulman, p. 56
Joint Distribution Committee, p. 58
Jerusalem, Sir Isaac and Lady Wolfson Museum, p. 61, 101;
        color: pl. 2, 6, 8 (top)
Jerusalem, Jewish Agency Photo Service, p. 62
New York, Jewish Museum, p. 65, 101
Munich, Staatsbibliothek, p. 65
B. Picart, *Ceremonies et Coutumes Religieuses,* 1723, p. 68
Jerusalem, B.M. Ansbacher Collection, p. 72, 77, 80
London, Mocatta Library, p. 76
Washington, Library of Congress, p. 85
Darmstadt, Hessiche Landes-und Hochschulbibliothek, p. 86
Sarajevo, National Museum, p. 87, 95
Photo H. Burger, Jerusalem, p. 90, 107
New York, Siegfried Bendheim Collection, p. 90
New York, Congregation Shearith Israel, p. 93
B. Tsedaka, Holon, p. 97
Formerly Letchworth, England, Sassoon Collection, p. 103
Manchester, John Rylands Library, pl. 4
New York, Central Synagogue of New York, pl. 7
Cleveland, Joseph B. and Olyn Horwitz Collection, pl. 8 (bottom)
Photo J. Goren, Jerusalem, pl. 3
Cover: Delft *seder* dish by Albrest de Kerser, 1642.

120